MW00626857

Curtain Call is an exp̲ ̲ ̲ ̲ ̲ reminds us of three ̲ ̲ ̲ ̲ ̲ ̲ ̲ surprising journey, each of us has experienced grief, and, even so, there is always hope for our future. Lyneta Smith reaches into her heart, baring her story with brisk honesty and unflinching candor. Beautiful writing, exquisite storytelling.

Mary DeMuth, author of *Thin Places: A Memoir*

How do the adults of our childhood construct the very adult we grow up to be? Lyneta Smith's story of learning the truth about the people who raised her, and the God who loved her, is gut-wrenching and hope-giving all at the same time.

Kathi Lipp – bestselling author of *Clutter Free Home* and *Ready for Anything*

Curtain Call by Lyneta Smith is an unforgettable memoir. As Ms. Smith relates her painful stories of childhood abuse and the equally heart-rending neglect of a cold and distant mother, I ached for the pain of the secrets she was forced to keep. They were secrets that returned to plague her as an adult, forcing her to deal with her past as it began to affect her relationships in the present.

Throughout this memoir, Ms. Smith does a masterful job of interspersing the stories of her childhood with her adulthood. While the descriptions of the abuse were clear, they were never presented in an offensive manner to the reader. Rather, you could feel the emotional and physical pain of each encounter, while being equally horrified by her mother's verbal abuse and lack of maternal protection.

But this memoir does not present just the pain but reveals the author's hope as she was able to attain help through counselling. Ultimately, her healing came through her faith in a God who loves her and chose her to help others through her story. She learned that she is loved and valued for the person she is. And that painful secrets can cripple emotionally when they are not dealt with.

Bravo to Ms. Smith for her bravery in opening the door to her painful secrets. In so doing, she has discovered many others who now feel the freedom to sever the chains of their own prison of fear. She will help bring healing to many through her own recovery.

Elaine Marie Cooper, award-winning author of *Fields of the Fatherless*, *Bethany's Calendar*, *Saratoga Letters*

Curtain Call

A memoir

LYNETA SMITH

Curtain Call
Copyright ©2020
Lyneta Smith

ISBN: 978-0-578-81352-3 (paperback)
       978-1-7362426-0-5 (ebook)

Second edition. First edition published March 19, 2019

Published by Hand 'n Hand Press
676 W. Pullman Road Suite 332
Moscow, ID 83843
www.handnhand.press

Dedication

For every silent survivor
You are not alone

Contents

Chapter One

In 2014, I wanted out of my story. If I could've rewritten the script, I would have gladly done so. This wasn't the show I'd auditioned for. This life I'd always wanted was not enough.

I was not enough.

Only during sleep could I escape the frantic need to be more.

My husband's alarm blared from across the room of our suburban Spring Hill, Tennessee home, startling me out of a deep sleep. He swung his feet over the bed and stumbled toward the dresser. By the time he turned off the beeping, I was wide awake, despite dropping into bed, bleary-eyed, at 2:00 a.m., after typing a political science paper due the next day. At forty-two, all-nighters were harder to pull off than in my high school days.

Doug sat on the bed with a bounce, his white t-shirt visible by the streetlight pouring into the window. I rubbed his back, savoring the feel of soft cotton. He patted my arm. Very little time for snuggling or even conversation these days.

5:00 a.m. No sleeping in today. Too much to do to. I'd put everything else off until after my deadline, and now it was time to catch up.

In the kitchen, I scooped coffee grounds into the filter, adding a couple extra tablespoons. It was going to take a lot for my brain fog to float away. I gathered my Bible and notebook and plunked them onto the table.

"Please help me accomplish everything I need to do today," I asked God. Between my job as Oregon State's online writing lab coordinator, my coursework, and homeschooling my youngest daughter in her senior year, I had to keep a list of my to-do lists.

After Doug left for his computer programming job at Dave Ramsey's office, I trudged upstairs, second cup of coffee in hand, ready to knock out my job, then start my schoolwork. If I could just keep up this pace for another term...*summa cum laude*, here I come.

For what that was worth. Despite all the political science and pre-law classes—and weeks of practice tests—I'd only gotten a 150 on the LSAT. Average. No chance of getting into Vanderbilt Law with that. I'd have to go to a state school, and that meant moving to another town. Not an option.

All my hard work, and I was still unprepared for what I thought I wanted.

Admitting that after graduation I would not be applying to law school wasn't easy, but I couldn't even think about three more years of school, followed by being chained to a desk twelve to fourteen hours a day just to get my career started. Surprisingly, letting go of that shadow mission felt like unloading a burden I didn't know I carried.

What I didn't realize then was that a law degree would have only been one more façade among many to make me "estimable," "exceptional," i.e., capable of changing the world.

Someone worthy of love.

If I could only keep working hard enough, make enough people believe enough, then I would finally *become* enough.

Graduating with honors as the first bachelor's degree holder in my family would be my undeniable proof.

But now, that old feeling was creeping back in again. Deep down, I knew I was invisible, ill-prepared, and insignificant.

This is madness.

I felt my way onto the dark stage and wiped my damp palms on a borrowed, drab skirt. I had no idea if I was standing in the right place, but when the lights came on, I sang the familiar *Fiddler on the Roof* lyrics to "Sunrise, Sunset," trying to follow the rest of the cast.

Though my untrained voice lacked confidence, I plastered a sincere look of pride and bittersweet celebration on my face, as though I'd watched Tzeitel and Motel grow from birth in our impoverished Russian village.

"Mazel tov!" we shouted as Motel crushed a wine glass under his heel. Backstage, someone on the crew stomped on already-broken glass inside a wooden box to amplify the sound. I pretended to know exactly what to do in my revelry, while I prayed the scene would end so I could slip backstage.

At last, the cue for the last scene came. I trekked across the stage with the Jewish villagers leaving Anatevka. We carried our few belongings in empty, beat-up leather bags. On our slow, sad trek across stage, we shivered and pulled our ratty grey and brown wool coats tighter to ward off the frigid winter air while perspiration dripped down our backs under the hot stage lights.

After the last scene, I joined the rest of the chorus onstage for curtain call. We lined up, grasped hands, and rushed to the front to give our bows. A rush of pleasure carried me through the applause, their appreciation growing louder as the principle actors took their bows. I breathed relief as we rushed offstage.

I'd never auditioned for *Fiddler on the Roof*, or any other production. My role as a backstage mom suited me well. I could braid six or seven heads of hair and do makeup before the show and keep an eye on my girls.

But that year, an epidemic hit our little town. After the first week's knockout performance, a nasty virus spread through the small space we shared in the dressing rooms. Many cast members called in sick, and even some who didn't should have. I witnessed Frumah Sarah burst into the dressing room directly after the flying scene and run to a toilet stall, where she spent the rest of Act I throwing up. The director desperately sought replacements.

The day before I found myself floundering onto a dark stage, the director caught up with me in the green room. Her vivacious personality commanded attention everywhere she went. She had a knack for inspiring the cast to work hard and give their best, all the while having the time of their lives. I beamed as she complimented me on my help backstage.

She laid her hand on my shoulder. "You could be in the show, you know."

I took a step backward. "Me? No, I'm more of a back—"

She stepped forward and looked me intently in the eyes. "I really need you to be in the chorus."

My eyes widened. "But, I haven't rehearsed!"

"You've been here for every rehearsal, though. You probably know it better than I do."

I had been present for my young daughters, even sewed a half dozen peasant blouses for the cast, but that didn't mean I could dance and sing in front of 500 people.

I took a step backward. "How do you even know I can sing?"

"Okay, let's try it." She started singing the melody of "Tradition" in her beautiful alto voice and motioned with her hand for me to join her. I floundered through the chorus along with her.

"See, you've got it!" She patted me on the arm and slipped away. Over her shoulder she said, "Go to Pat in the costume shop and make sure you have a blouse and skirt."

Me, onstage? My two youngest daughters, then eight and eleven years old, had rehearsed for weeks, learning choreography and lyrics with the cast of seventy-five. They'd worked too hard for the show to tank, just because there weren't enough cast members.

And that's how I found myself in the middle of a scene I'd never rehearsed.

After my first show, with sweat-soaked peasant blouse and streaked makeup, I bumped into the director. "Was I okay?"

"What do you mean?" She balanced her three-ring binder and water jug as we slipped by each other in the hallway.

Please tell me I did great, and that you appreciated the horror I just went through. "Did I do what you wanted me to do?"

"Well, I didn't see anything out of place, so you must have."

I nodded and moved down the hallway. She hadn't even seen me.

My shoulders slumped a little but I'm not sure what I'd expected. *Only three more performances left in the week,* I told myself. *Hopefully the other actors will be well by next week.* I pushed open the heavy door to the dressing room, knowing it wouldn't be the last time I felt invisible. Nor was it the first.

As a three-year-old, I walked up the sagging wooden steps to our house in Pinedale, Wyoming, a small town near the Teton Mountains.

Time to see Daddy! In the three long days I had stayed with my grandma and grandpa across town, I had many unanswered questions.

"Why can't we go home?" I'd asked. "Where's Daddy?" It had seemed my mom and grandparents couldn't answer.

But today would be a good day.

As we walked up, my dad came out onto the front porch. I smiled big and ran to greet him, but I stopped short when I saw his face. He looked mad. Really mad.

It was like I wasn't even there. He and Mom were yelling at each other.

Before I could figure out what was happening, he was over behind the woodpile, grabbing his gun. "Git!"

Wait, I thought we would get to play together!

I stood next to Mom, who held Monte, my infant brother. *What is happening?*

Dad lifted the long barrel into the air and fired. A loud crack rang out.

Mom pushed us back into her faded red Ford Galaxie. As we backed out of the driveway, he was holding the rifle in one hand and pushing on the car hood with the other, like he wanted to make us go away faster.

Didn't he see me?

Didn't he see how I wanted to hug him and tell him how much I missed him?

The next days I spent in grief and confusion. No one would explain Daddy's anger, or why we couldn't go back home. Back at my grandparent's house, a police officer stood in the kitchen. I stared, taking in his shiny boots, dark brown pants, and the golden badge on his chest. "I'll see you in ten days," he said as he headed out the door. He hadn't even glanced my way.

From listening to whispers, I figured out that my daddy had been in jail. Did he get out? Maybe he was getting out in ten days, and that's what the police officer was talking about. Later on, I overheard Grandma telling my mom that she couldn't borrow their Chevy Suburban. "We can't let you park it in front of that house. What will people think?"

The next time I saw my dad, we sat on the couch together while Mom gathered stuff from the bedrooms and kitchen. We drove off without him.

After a seven-hour drive, we finally arrived in our new town. I sat in front, taking in all the huge stores and houses. So many houses, it seemed like they went on forever.

Suddenly, Mom slammed on the brakes and I lurched forward, smashing my face into the front windshield.

I cried a panicked, frantic cry. The taste of blood nauseated me.

Mom pulled me back into the seat. The corners of her mouth turned down as she pulled hair away from my face. "Let me look at it."

She glanced at the stoplight. "Quit crying."

Trying to stifle my sobs, I held my mouth with my hand. Blood and snot covered my face and fingers.

When the light turned green, Mom continued the short distance the rest of the way to our relatives' house. I leaned my head back against the leather seat.

When we arrived, people I had never met offered cold washcloths, helped me clean up, and settled us into a house I'd never seen. I sat silently amidst all the talking and unloading of bags. Did Mom mean for us to stay in this new strange place? How long?

I entered the first major change in my life much like my first musical production—unprepared and feeling my way in the dark. Like the Russian peasants leaving Anatevka, I had no idea what the future held. And I could only guess whether there was any way back home.

Chapter Two

December 2013, Spring Hill, Tennessee

But that was ages ago. And I'd certainly arrived home now. *Right?*

I glanced around our bonus room at three happy girls still in Christmas Eve pajamas, ripping green and red paper off the boxes Doug and I had spent a week wrapping. Though all of the girls had surpassed me in height, none of us could give up the traditions we'd cherished from their younger years.

Every Christmas morning, we gathered around the tree, laden with the girls' homemade works of art and memento ornaments. It was Katie's job, as the youngest and most energetic, to hand out gifts.

She brought me a large, flat box with a legal-sized envelope taped to it. I started to open it, but Doug stopped me. "No, open the present first."

"Really? Okay." It went against our tradition of opening the card first for any gift-giving occasion, but in no time, I'd torn off the paper.

I held up a large, black-framed piece of original art. Two ladies hugged next to a suitcase with a river, mountains, and trees in the background.

"This is great! Thank you!" *Artwork? I should have been more specific with my Christmas wish list.* I smiled at Doug and turned the picture around for everyone else to see.

"What do you think it is?" Doug's expectant grin told me there was a lot more to this present than something to hang on the wall.

I looked at it again. "It's two friends. They're happy to see each other. But it's two girls, so not you and me, right?"

"Right. And where are they?"

I sighed. All of the girls had puzzled expressions, so he hadn't clued them in either. I looked at my half-empty coffee cup. In our haste to get to the presents, I hadn't had my normal two mugs to shake off the fogginess.

I shook my head. "Camping?"

Doug's smile shortened slightly. "Open the envelope."

I pulled out the page and read aloud. "Southwest Airlines? To PDX?"

Doug looked pleased as punch. "Yep."

"For me?"

He nodded.

The girls all exclaimed at once. "Wow, you get to go to Portland? Lucky!"

I continued to soak in the details. "December 27th? That's in two days!"

Doug filled me in on the plan. I'd be staying with my longtime friend and mentor Patti in Oregon City for a few days over Christmas break, and so would a few of my other girlfriends who still lived in Newport. They'd secretly been planning it for a couple months.

After the excitement died down, we continued our unwrapping. Amidst the shouts of, "Thank you! Just what I wanted!" and "Cool, look what I got!" a smidgen of dread trickled in.

Why does the thought of getting on a plane and traveling across the country sound as daunting as climbing Mt. Hood?

It was the first time since we'd moved to Tennessee that my spirit hadn't leaped in excitement for the chance to visit our friends and family. *I should be more excited about this. How am I going to get the energy in just two short days?*

After we'd thrown all the paper and ribbons away, I hugged my epic gift-giver tight and thanked him. "You're the best husband ever."

He smiled, obviously pleased to have pulled off such a big surprise. Down inside, I steeled myself to pack for the weekend and be happy during my girls' weekend.

During winter term, my spirit sagged like the dreary, cold weather. Though my short stay at Patti's temporarily boosted my spirits, I fell right back into my grindstone-busy routine when winter term started.

As a writing student, I thought I would look forward to reading and evaluating fiction, a much welcome change from political science and history classes I'd been taking in anticipation of law school. Study the elements of literature so I could be a better writer.

I got more than I bargained for.

One of my professors assigned "Trains," by Alice Munro. I sprawled out across my bed sideways to read it.

In the story, a man named Jackson travels back from the war on a train. His fiancé waits for him in his hometown, but he makes the surprising decision to jump off the slow-moving train before reaching his destination.

I read on, curious to know why he returned safe from the war, only to abandon his fiancé without a word and then avoid romantic relationships throughout his itinerant life.

Finally, on the last page, I discovered what it was that made his heart impenetrable. He said, "Things could be locked up; it only took some determination." I gripped the book, heart racing.

"Things," I learned, were that his stepmother had fondled him in the bathtub when he was very young.

I tossed the book off the edge of the bed like a hot potato. My face felt hot and tears sprung to my eyes. At the time, I had no idea why the story affected me so deeply, why I was so hurt for this fictional little boy, who'd never escaped the indignity, no matter how far he ran.

During an online class discussion about "Trains," I expressed my revulsion for the thematic content, but couldn't find any other criticisms for the author. It was a well-written story with an engaging plot and true to life characters. *Maybe a little too well-written.*

Not all of my professors had the same commitment to teaching from excellent literature. In another class, I was forced to read a detective novel so horribly written that my thesis statement facetiously argued that it's not possible for anyone to write so badly, except on purpose. I reasoned that the author must have been making fun of detective novels in general by grossly exaggerating common detective novel elements and ignoring anything resembling good writing technique.

One of these awful elements included graphic sex scenes written almost kindergarten-like and pasted into spots that didn't make sense. What had started out as a sensible plot structure in the beginning deteriorated to nonsensical.

I hoped my scathing essay would anger the teacher enough to give me my first F ever. I'd print out my grade and his comments and fasten it to my cork bulletin board next to my desk like a certificate of honors.

But I didn't get an F.

I got far worse than an F.

It was a B. The teacher had made only one remark: "The elements you included were well-defined, thorough, and you listed plenty of examples. However, you didn't flesh out the use of sex scenes in the novel."

I showed Doug my grade. "How can I get a B?"

Having already heard about my hatred for the book more than once, he put his arms around me, as if to hold off a torrent of words. "It's just one assignment. You'll probably still get an A in the class."

"I know, but I wanted to make a statement. I should have stopped reading the book and written a respectful email explaining why I had to refuse the assignment. A zero would have been better than a B."

No matter how hard I tried to shut out the awful images I'd read, both in Alice Munro's "Trains," and the botched detective novel, I couldn't stop thinking about them.

And then, unbidden, another scene ran through my mind.

I watched in slow motion, helpless to stop it, much like one witnesses a car crash. But this time, it wasn't some figment of a writer's imagination. It was really happening. And the girl in that scene was me.

After my parents' divorce, we lived in a one-bedroom apartment in Buffalo. Most mornings, Mom slept late after a swing shift as a nurse's aid. We weren't allowed to go outside, so my brother and I entertained ourselves in the bedroom, careful not to make too much noise.

In the afternoons, Mom drove us to a pink house on a hill where the babysitter lived.

About six other kids besides my brother and me came to her house, including her nephew, who lived next door. A few years older, he towered over me. When he was there, he was the boss—the rest of us did what he said.

As much as I tried to avoid him, he found ways to make me miserable. I knew I was in for a rough day when he greeted me with, "Hey, Lie-NEE-tuh Pie-PEE-tuh." The others followed his lead.

Without even acknowledging the slam on my name, Mom would walk out the door, leaving me to fend for myself. If I tried to complain about my treatment there, she'd only say, "Oh, quit tattling."

If I shed tears while watching her drive away out the window, the babysitter lectured me about being selfish. "Oh, grow up. Your mom has to go to work so she can feed you and give you a place to live." Every morning I would pray it was Mom's day off. If I saw her getting ready for work, my heart raced a little faster, and I'd try to think up ways to make my time at the babysitter's more bearable.

One day, to my relief, Mom said she wasn't getting ready for work. Not that day, nor the next.

"Tomorrow's a day off?"

"Yep." Mom unrolled the curling iron and let a curly brown lock fall around her face.

"And the next day?"

"Yep. A week off."

A whole week without going to the babysitter's? I squealed with delight and skipped around our little apartment. What could I do? Play outside in the grass, maybe even pet the neighbor's puppy.

Or maybe Mom would take us to the visit the nursing home where she worked. Sometimes a lady with a wrinkled face and puffy lips would be sitting in the lobby. The only thing I ever heard her say was, "Oh, Children! I love children." She always kissed my hand and gave me a little chewy candy. I didn't really like her big lips touching my hand, but getting the candy was worth it.

Later, I passed by Mom talking on the phone, my sock monkey dangling under my arm. One of her patients had made my brother and I each one. I heard her say goodbye, then she hung up. "Get your shoes. We're going."

"Where?"

"You're going to spend the night at the babysitter's."

No! "But you said you had the day off." My stomach twisted into knots. "We're going to stay the night?"

She explained that she and a friend were going to Canada "just to say they had" and that she'd pick my brother and I up late the next evening.

Please God, don't let *him* be there. The babysitter's nephew. Dread crept up into my throat and squeezed. I fought off the panic by telling myself he wasn't there every day. Maybe not this time.

I was beginning to believe that everything in life turned out like I feared, and this day was no exception. He was there.

My heart thumped a little faster when I saw him and his cousins, another nephew and a niece. From the looks they shot me, I could already tell it wasn't going to be a nice two days.

Before long, the babysitter pushed us outside. "Go play!"

The yard, a giant dirt patch enclosed in chain link, had a swing set and merry-go-round installed, but very few other toys.

Her nephew would only allow me on the swing set if I took the double dog dare: go as high as I can and jump off when it was as high as it would go. There were six of us, but only three swings. If I ever wanted a turn, I'd have to do what he said.

When the swing's chain jerked, I knew my time was up. The nephew and the others yelled at me to jump off, so I unwrapped my arms from the chain and launched forward, landing in the dirt with a thud. Stinging and bloody, I sat in front of the still-in-motion swing, fighting back the tears.

"Aw, look. She's crying." Nephew and his cousins rallied the other kids to taunt. "Crybaby."

I already knew better than to "go tell." That hadn't gone well the last time I'd tried it. The babysitter had punished me by making me stand with my nose in a corner for what seemed like hours. "Maybe now you'll learn not to be a tattletale," she'd said.

I brushed the dirt off the best I could, deciding to be content with staying off "their" playground equipment.

That wasn't the worst day. Another time, the three cousins decided we would all play "rodeo." Since the merry-go-round had four seats, we'd all take turns. There were three horses and one "bull," the seat where the horse head had fallen off. Since it had no handles, the oldest nephew found a rope.

"If you want to ride, you have to get on the bull," he told me.

No problem. I'd ridden that one before. I'd just grip both sides of the seat.

The nephew had other plans, though. "No, you tie your hand on." He wrapped the rope around and around the seat with my hand on top. "Now, put your other hand in the air."

The girl cousin sat across from me, gripping the handles on her horse head. Nephew pushed the merry-go-round faster and faster. I stretched my other hand as high as it would go, but the spin lasted much longer than eight seconds. I soon figured out that he did not intend to stop the merry-go-round. I wailed to get off.

"You're a bull rider. You have to jump!"

Again, I landed in the dirt. I swallowed a lump in my throat. They could laugh at me, but they wouldn't catch me crying this time. They might see the bruises and cuts on my elbows and knees, but not the ones on my heart.

On bad weather days, the nephew and his followers at least made pretense of being a little nicer. In the babysitter's hearing, they weren't too mean. But sometimes if the bigger kids were out of school for some reason, she sent us downstairs. The uncarpeted staircase led to a big room with concrete walls.

Though full of toys (mostly baby toys), and a couple of beds, there wasn't a lot to do. We usually made up our own games. None of us ever had to think too hard, though, since the nephew dictated them anyway.

One of those rainy days, all three cousins and I, along with some other kids, played "Follow the Leader" downstairs. As usual, the nephew was the leader. The rest of us trailed behind him in line, picking up an item and dropping it, then doing jumping jacks, and repeating silly phrases.

He turned and said, "Okay, we're going to do something different."

The rest of us circled around to hear about the new game. "We're gonna play house. I'm the dad, so you do what I say."

Of course.

"You." He pointed to me. "Come here."

I slowly made my way over to where he stood by the bed.

"Pull down your pants." He stood over me, staring with squinty eyes and scrunched up lips.

I didn't know what would happen if I didn't do what he said. It usually ended up making things worse if I didn't. I shook my head no.

"Yes. You have to."

Would he hurt me? The rest of the kids had gathered around.

When I did, he ordered me to lie down on the bed. With everyone watching, he hunted around and picked up a baby toy. I didn't really know what he was doing, but a sharp pain hit I'd never felt before. Much worse than the sting of soap when Mom would wash me at bath time.

"Stop!" I didn't care if they saw me crying this time. "Quit it!" My loud voice scared even me.

He looked toward the open door leading toward the stairway. "Okay, you big baby." He let me up. "Fine. I won't do it."

I let out a shaky breath and stood up. Was it really over?

"Crybaby." He crossed his arms and frowned at me.

The others stood staring, knowing they'd encountered something new and strange.

"Don't tell anyone, or I'll do it even worse." He glowered at me as I fastened my pants and dried my tears.

Who would I tell, anyway? The babysitter would put me in the corner for tattling. My mom wouldn't listen.

It was my secret for almost twenty years before I told anyone.

I was grown, married, and pregnant with my first daughter. As a first-time mother and a member of the Air Force, I had spent hours researching daycare options. Even thinking about leaving my little one made my stomach queasy. I had a year of active duty left after my due date, so I had to find someone to watch her.

In the midst of this, Mom called with the news to tell me that someone from our old hometown had been stationed at

Fairchild AFB, same as me.

My old babysitter's nephew.

She urged me to call him, because she'd told his mom and grandmother I would be sure to.

"No, I'm not going to."

"Why not?" Her tone of voice issued more of a challenge rather than curiosity.

I spilled how he'd treated me, including the molestation. "Why did you send me to that awful babysitter's anyway?" I asked.

"I didn't have anyone else to send you to."

She said nothing about the bullying or the rape in the basement. "Anyway, I told the family I would have you call him. So make sure you do it, okay?"

I sighed. "Okay, Mom." With a little luck, she'd forget about it and wouldn't nag me anymore. Maybe it was right to call him, like they said. We had known each other as kids. I wondered if I were wrong to make such a big deal about it. It had been a long time ago.

Though I copied down the number she gave me, I never ended up calling him. I let all thoughts of him slip away as I navigated motherhood, a career, and a rocky marriage.

One day, while standing at a lunch counter on base with a male coworker, I heard my name. My first name—pronounced correctly. *Ly NEE tuh.* Most people called me by my married surname in the military. I turned around in surprise.

The nephew stood behind us. "Hey, I heard you were here. I was going to call you guys." He glanced between coworker's face and mine.

He must have thought my coworker was my new husband. I made no introductions. Thankfully, at that moment the server handed my coworker and me brown paper bags with tuna sandwiches and Lay's chips and then asked for nephew's order. I took the opportunity to make a quick exit.

"Hey, what's your hurry?" My coworker chased after me as the glass door swung closed behind me. He pushed it open again and followed me as we half-jogged to the truck. "What's wrong?"

"Nothing." *Nothing anyone cares to hear, anyway.* I climbed into the passenger seat and slammed the truck door closed, as if to put a lid on the memories crawling around in a deep, dark hole. Ugly, nasty little things.

When the curtain fell on the stream of memories, I slowly pulled my mind into the present. My heart thumped wildly, as if I had just climbed the cement steps up to the babysitter's house. My stomach threatened to hurl the two cups of coffee I'd drunk.

Just then, the phone rang. It was Doug. "How was your morning?"

I looked around at my desk, covered by mountains of textbooks and various clutter. "Good. Busy." I was behind on my writing lab work and needed to get started on my own classwork. "How's your day?"

I kept asking him question after question. He'd made a habit of calling for about ten minutes on his lunch hour every day. Better to keep the topic of conversation on his day rather than mine.

But I only half-listened. *Where had those memories come from?* I hadn't thought about the bully in the basement since Mariah was a baby.

After Doug hung up, I downloaded a file and set to work critiquing a student paper. I didn't have time to worry about the past. Couldn't change it anyway. And I sure as heck wasn't going to tell anyone. That part of me was best kept closed.

In theatre, one of the first things a new actor learns is not to ruin the magic of the show. I got my first peek into all the rules and etiquette of theatre during that first show in Newport, Oregon, from our involvement with Coastal Act Production's *Fiddler on the Roof*. Director Kim Fiske stood on the front stage in the auditorium where Mariah and Katie would perform in two short days, addressing the elementary and middle school actors.

"I don't want to see you waving to your mom, or even looking at the audience. This isn't a school play. It's a community theatre production." She animated each action with exaggerated waves and stares and we all chuckled.

"Oh, and one more thing. Never, ever peek through these curtains when the house is open." She pointed behind her to the burgundy curtains, which hung regally from the ten-foot ceiling. "If I see you do it, I can guarantee you won't be in the next show."

The memories had come like an errant, juvenile actor, who couldn't resist the urge to see the auditorium filled with an audience before the curtains opened. They threatened to ruin the magic.

I'd worked too hard to create a happy, Christian home. I wanted to be the happy, healthy homeschooling mom, not the helpless little girl, crying in the babysitter's basement. No way would I accept the role of abuse victim. That character would never be part of my show.

Lyneta Smith

Chapter Three

January 2014—Spring Hill, Tennessee

Are you okay?

The question came from within me somewhere, something like the adult me checking in on a trembling, sniffling little girl.

Yeah...I guess. I shook my head.

Great. Now I'm having conversations with myself. I don't have time for this.

I squirted cleanser all over the bathroom counter and double sinks and scrubbed away the grime, as if to scrub away the crazy. I really needed to hold it together.

But the memories wouldn't stop coming. One by one, they ran through like scenes in my mind, sometimes more than once. Long-forgotten but familiar, it was almost like watching another person's life in their skin.

My phone buzzed with a text from Doug.

"Are we all having dinner together before our church small group tonight?"

"Yes," I typed back. *But I'm not going to small group.*

Much as I wanted the approval of those couples, I would find a reason to weasel out.

I stowed the cleaning supplies in the cupboard and headed for the kitchen. After pouring a cup of coffee, I logged on to Facebook. One of my *Music Man* friends had posted a heartfelt plea for help.

"I feel like I'm slogging through cement. How do I get out of this hole?"

Her words mirrored what I longed to say. I would have never had the courage to type them, though.

I hadn't known her long. We only did one show together before she moved away to another state. But I did understand the dark place from where she cried out.

I typed a comment on her post. "Don't forget that it never looks good for the heroine when the curtain goes down at intermission. Hang on to hope that it'll eventually be better in the second act."

The dryer buzzed, jolting me back to reality. I gulped down the rest of my coffee and rushed to finish laundry so I could work on school. It would be another long night of papers to write and assignments to complete. I couldn't slack off now. *Summa cum laude* was just within my grasp.

As I poured bleach into the washer, another wave of memories bubbled its way to the surface. I could almost smell beach and urine soaking in a cloth diaper pail, the one sitting in the bedroom of that one bedroom apartment in Buffalo.

All of the snow had melted away that morning I spotted my daddy's green pickup parked by the curb. He was inside! I ran out into the street to the driver's side door. As he got out to greet me, I leaped into his arms. *I never thought I'd get to see you again.*

He pulled me into a big embrace. His chest was warm and I could feel the thump of his heartbeat. He chuckled, a low rumble that made his Adam's apple vibrate. Finally, he put me down and pulled something from behind the bench seat. "Happy Easter."

It was a purple bunny, the blow-up kind. He blew it up for me and sealed it. I clutched it in one hand and held one of his pointer fingers with the other as we walked into the apartment. For days, I didn't let him out of my sight. When he sat, I perched on his lap. If he was up doing something, I stuck right by his side.

When Mom got home from work, we showed her the new thing he taught me. I had practiced writing my name on a chalkboard with an easel frame over and over.

My parents put a mattress on the bedroom floor for my brother and I to share, and they slept in the bed. Eventually, he had to go to work again, so I had to go to the babysitter's, but the bullying didn't bother me as much anymore. I had my daddy back.

Not long after, we moved into a three-bedroom house on top of the hill, and I started kindergarten. My brother and I shared a bedroom, but Mom and Dad had their own. Dad took a job cutting trees for a timber company, which meant he stayed up on the mountain for days at a time.

One afternoon, I sat on my bed while my mother towered over me, her eyes wide and nostrils flaring. Her gravelly voice croaked from so much yelling.

I had been bad. Again. And whatever I'd done this time, it must have been awful because there was no sign of her letting up.

"I'm going to put you down in that basement!"

I looked where she was pointing, past the kitchen and through the open door to the laundry room. The linoleum floor had a hinged-trap door as wide and long as a regular door. I'd peeked down once when my parents had it open. Creaky wooden stairs led to a dirt floor, and the dimly lit by a bare bulb hanging.

As Dad climbed back up the stairs, he'd seen me leaning over the side. "You don't want to get too close, now."

Then he'd closed the door with a thud.

Even if I'd pulled with all my might, I couldn't have opened that door. There was no way I'd want to go down there, especially by myself.

Mom wasn't nearly finished. "That's where the devil lives, and you belong down there with him because you're such a brat!"

She stomped out and slammed my bedroom door, and visions of "devil" and hellfire flared in my imagination. I'd seen the devil on *The Bugs Bunny Show* in a red suit and carrying a pitchfork, and I didn't want to encounter him anywhere.

I scooted back until I sat against the wall and clutched my pillow to my chest. Did the devil really live in our basement? What if Mom did put me down there? Would I be burned up? I had nightmares about being trapped in the basement and trying to hide from a devil.

When Dad was home, he tucked me in. "Snug as a bug in a rug." I tried every stall tactic I could think of to stay up later, but Dad would only say, "Tomorrow's another day." Each night I'd beg, "Please leave the door open a crack?"

At least the pinch of light from the living room could chase away whatever my imagination conjured up about hell in the darkness.

I listened to the muffled sounds of television from my room. My parents watched *Fantasy Island*, *MASH*, or *60 Minutes* as I counted off the day's events. How bad was I?

If I die in my sleep, will I go to heaven?

Maybe if I tried a little harder, I could be good enough to

get in.

In school, I excelled ahead of my peers academically since I could read, but I lagged behind in behavioral development. As a result, I was one of "those kids," the ones who got sent to time-out. Unfortunately for my poor teacher, my response to sitting in the time-out chair was more attitude. *This is all you've got?* That was nothing compared to what I was used to.

By the end of the year, she'd learned how to motivate me: praise. She heaped compliments and attention on me for advancing in reading. As I started to like her, I wanted to please her. She gave me more books to read at home. I already loved to climb onto Dad's lap and read my stack of Dr. Seuss, so adding extra reading assignments came naturally.

Mom and Dad made a big deal out of my success. Academic achievement became the way I could be loved.

I had been running from the devil ever since then. I worked and worked to keep my identity from being "the bad girl." On the outside, I looked like any other suburban Middle Tennessee mom filling her front loader, but on the inside I sat trembling on my bed, praying Mom wouldn't follow through on her threat to put me in the basement.

The question haunted me. *Why was I so bad?* If only I could be someone else—anyone else. What would happen if people knew me—the real me? Not the friend who gives good advice on Facebook and takes care of her family, but the one who hides from her commitments to the people of her church, skipping small group and wondering how a good God could let these horrible things happen.

"Please God?" I begged. "Can't I have a different life? One where I don't have to pretend? Anything would be better than this one."

Chapter Four

I looked out the passenger window as Doug drove the winding back road on the way to small group. Since the headlights only lit a short distance ahead, there wasn't much to see.

He glanced over at me. "I'm glad you're coming with me."

I wasn't. After skipping several weeks in a row, I reluctantly agreed to go with him. "Me too." I smiled, at least a half-smile.

"They're great people, you know." He reached for my hand and squeezed it.

"Yeah." True enough. But I had nothing in common with them. Even after three years, our appearance felt more like casual acquaintances crashing a family reunion. It was obvious by their conversations that they all interacted with each other throughout the week, so it was like we were stepping into a half-finished meeting.

I thought of the last time I'd been there. As I walked into the hostess's kitchen, she had boisterously greeted me with an outstretched arm, but mispronouncing my name. "Hey, *Lyn NĚT uh*. How are you?"

I decided not to correct her, since I'd already tried several times. "Fine, thank—"

Just then, she jerked her head to see who was just coming in the door.

"Andrea!" She pulled her arm away from what I assumed was meant to be a hug and slipped across the living room before I could even get a response out.

I'm invisible.

No one seemed to notice that I sat in silence for the rest of the evening, nor did they know when I slipped out the door without saying goodbye.

Doug pulled me from my thoughts. "You'd connect with them better if you'd only make an effort. You get out of it what you put into it, right?"

"I have *tried*. I'm not sure what else to do."

"Have you considered trying to reach out to them? Sometimes you have to be the one to take the initiative."

I pulled my hand away from his. "Really? Because one day I too can fit in with the Brentwood Barbies? Is that my goal?"

I was picking a fight, but I didn't care. Why should I pretend to be happy for people who didn't even seem to care whether I showed up or not? Let alone learning to pronounce my name.

Doug pulled into a well-lit parking lot in the gas station. We were almost to the small group leaders' house. He likely didn't want to be in the middle of an argument when we walked in the door.

"I'm just saying that you have isolated yourself lately."

"And *I'm just saying* that you have no idea what you're talking about. We've been going to that group for three years and the leader still doesn't even know my name!" The car seemed to be closing in on us.

Doug kept his voice even. "Sometimes it takes awhile."

"And *sometimes* people just don't give a crap. Even if we could afford the clothes, the expensive hairdressers, and all that other junk, is that who you want me to be? Someone who spends too much to impress people I don't even like?" I was yelling, the surest way to shut down an argument with the man who doesn't love confrontations.

Doug clenched the steering wheel with his left hand and put the car in reverse in the other. He pulled out onto the highway again, but turned the car back the way we'd come, toward home.

Good.

"You can blame everyone else for your problems, but nothing's going to get better unless you open up to someone."

"I'm not blaming them for anything. I just hate going to this small group." I wasn't sure why he was so dedicated. It wasn't like he had any relationship with them outside the group. "You don't click with them either." The tone in my voice could have melted glass.

"Then find people you do click with. Instead of being on Facebook all the time, get out and make some real friends."

Adrenaline shot through me. Who was he to tell me that I wasn't trying hard enough. I worked hard every day, all day. "In all my spare time? Should I just quit my job and drop my classes? You never wanted me to go to school in the first place!"

He took a deep breath. "If you don't stop yelling at me, I'm going to pull this car over and walk home by myself." It was a rare time when he raised his voice.

Fine. I crossed my arms and pursed my lips. I didn't want to talk about it anymore anyway. Especially not Facebook. Again.

I watched tree shadows out the passenger side window as Doug navigated the curves.

"You want to find another small group? Is that it?"

I couldn't think of one person in the entire church that I wanted to see every week. It was hard enough to sit through an hour and a half of worship and sermon on Sundays. "Just stop."

"Why won't you talk to me?"

"I am talking to you."

"You know what I mean." He sighed. "You can do what you've been doing and keep your nose to the grindstone. But if you keep isolating yourself, you won't ever have any friends."

"If you think these people are so great, why don't you go to small group by yourself? I'm tired of pretending a 'New Testament model for relationships' actually facilitates real friendships and support!" I made air quotes around the church's newest catchphrase.

"Will you stop making excuses?" With every volley, our voices grew louder.

Oh, yes. Yes, I would. In fact, I'd stop making any sort of conversation altogether. "Let me out right here. I'll walk home."

"You can't walk from here. It's not safe." Doug turned from the highway onto the road that led to our house. We were three miles away.

"Yes, I can. Let me out."

"No."

"Pull over this car right now!"

"I'm not going to let you out here in the dark. It's not safe on this road."

"Then turn into that subdivision." I pointed to a neighborhood where our friends, the Caseys lived.

His voice turned to scoffing. "Are you going to go to the Casey's house?"

"None of your business." He could park the car in there and let me out without stopping traffic on the main road.

"I'm not going to drop you off in the dark." He passed their subdivision.

"You are holding me in this car against my will! Let me out right now!"

"We're almost home."

"I *know* where we are."

He didn't respond.

"You think I can't get out of this car?"

As we approached a traffic light, it turned red. I hooked my finger around the door handle as Doug glided to a stop. He looked straight ahead. Out of the corner of my eye, I could see his body tense and rigid, gripping the steering wheel as if he could steer this train-wreck of an argument back into rational conversation.

I stared at the light. Did I really want to walk two miles in the dark and the frigid weather? I had on regular shoes, not boots, and no hat or gloves with me. It would take at least an hour, and there was barely any shoulder on the road.

We sat in silence as the other cars on the cross street pulled out and drove away. My heart pounded wildly and breaths came quick and shallow.

The light turned green. Doug breathed a sigh of relief while his body relaxed into a natural driving position.

We drove the rest of the way home in silence. Without a word, I got ready for bed and climbed in with a book. He didn't come to bed until I was long asleep.

It was still dark the next morning when we got up to prepare for the day. I could barely make out his face by the light of his cell phone as he texted someone. I slipped between him and the dresser toward the bedroom door.

"I'm going to see Aaron," he said. "Will you come with me?"

I stopped, then turned back to face him. He was still staring at his phone. I didn't really want to go see a counselor. But what else could we do? I didn't really want my marriage to end. I was stuck. "Sure."

My tone of voice likely didn't convince him I was optimistic, but at least I was willing. The thought of walking into that office launched a thousand butterflies in my stomach. Aaron, who'd helped us before with some communication issues in our marriage, was a nice guy, but I knew he wouldn't understand.

I thought of the time I'd gone by myself, trying to figure out why I sabotaged my efforts to lose weight and improve my health.

I had sat on the lumpy couch in his office and he sat across from me in an office chair, his leg crossed over his knee.

I was trying to explain some of my fears. "I had lost a lot of weight, and was feeling pretty good about myself, until, one day, an older man came up to me in the grocery store. He looked me up and down and said suggestively, 'Whoa, what's for dinner?'"

"An older guy?" Aaron's disgust registered on his face.

"Yeah, like late 50's, early 60's."

"And what did you do?"

"I just turned around and pushed my cart the other way. But what I'm afraid of is that if I lose the weight again, I'll have to deal with the same old junk."

Aaron waved his hand. "That won't happen."

At that point, I was honestly unsure whether Aaron was disgusted that an older man would say those things, or that he would say them to me, a disgusting person. Was he so sure it wouldn't happen again because I was approaching my late thirties?

If he hadn't gotten that, how would he understand my feelings now? But for Doug's sake, and because I felt guilty about the previous night's fight, I would go.

Aaron had moved to a bigger place since the last time we'd been to see him. Instead of one rickety couch crammed into a tiny space with his desk, we walked into a spacious office with a couch and several overstuffed chairs placed in a circle. The desk was off in the corner. Aaron sat in one of the chairs, and Doug and I settled onto the couch.

Doug and I sat flush up against each other, clutching hands. I determined not to let either of them into my inner thoughts, but I would listen to what Doug had to say.

"It's like she isn't here," he told Aaron. "When she's not working, she's sleeping. She just cuts herself off."

I couldn't deny it. But to turn the discussion away from any talk about what was hurting, I deflected to the fact that I don't trust people. It worked. We talked about that for the rest of the hour.

Aaron's Missouri accent and mild temperament put me at ease. "Listen, after all the years you've been with Doug, haven't you been able to trust him with a lot of things? You trust him with your girls."

I nodded.

"You trust him to work and make a living."

I kept nodding.

"You trust him with finances, and the house and all that?"

"Of course."

"Then maybe you could think about trusting him with this."

"Sure." *Nope. Never. I'll find a way to get past this on my own. I'm not going to be "that poor abused girl."* Just like I wasn't going to be the poor drunk's girl, or the poor anything. I'd built my world exactly how I wanted it, and whatever it took, I'd keep it.

But I missed my husband. Having such a big thing between us had eroded some of the closeness we once shared. Besides, even if he did know about my past, what could he do? What would he think of me?

One day, as I scrolled through Facebook, I noticed an advertisement for a book about childhood sexual abuse. The link featured an author I hadn't heard of before. She had a free quiz on her website about childhood abuse's effect on adulthood.

As I took the quiz, I noticed symptom after symptom, from overeating to constant headaches. A lot of my typical responses to circumstances were from an unexplainable anxiety, but I had never noticed that they were unhealthy ways of dealing with things. Other behaviors I had attributed to character deficiencies now made sense in light of unrecognized and unacknowledged damage caused before I could even tell the difference between right and wrong.

I found the book on Amazon and put it in my cart. There were several others on my wish list, so I added about five or six of those too. It was like buying Twinkies and a Coke at the grocery store—filling up the cart with kale, whole grain bread, and apples, hoping no one notices the junk when you check out. Maybe if I had enough other books in the order, no one would notice the book on sexual abuse.

I kept my new stash among the piles of political science and LSAT prep books that already lined my bedroom wall. Maybe I could fix this myself without having to talk to anyone about it. I'd read a few books, maybe join an anonymous group online, and find a way to deal with the memories. After all, I'd been fixing stuff from the time I was old enough to read.

"You don't treat books that way." My dad held up a nice

children's hardback, its front cover open to display the damage. I'd ripped the first page from bottom to about an inch from the top, with a penny-size hole in the center.

"You'll have to fix this." He handed it to me and left to rummage through the junk drawer in the kitchen.

I studied the book. How in the world would I fix this? In all my six years on the planet, I'd never been given such a task.

I stood in the living room, surrounded by a library of children's books all over the floor. He came back with a roll of clear tape and explained how to apply it to both sides of the page.

"What about this part?" I pointed at the hole in the center.

"Just leave it. You can't do anything about that." After I finished, he returned to inspect my handiwork.

"Is this good, Daddy?" I handed him the book. *Please don't be mad at me anymore. Tell me I'm not bad.*

"Yeah. You did a good job." He traced his finger along the line of tape on the page where I'd taped both sides. "Be careful with these from now on."

I would. That day I learned two things: books are sacred, and even a kindergartner can fix her messes.

Later, I used my skills to fix even bigger messes. As a talkative student, I often got into trouble for disrupting the class. The aptly named second grade teacher, Mrs. Cross, finally had enough.

She picked up the math packet I was supposed to be working on and flipped through the pages. "You'll need to finish this before you go to lunch."

My stomach growled as I tackled double-digit subtraction problems. *So many pages!* Soon, my classmates lined up to go to the lunchroom, but I still had two pages left. Mrs. Cross was the last one out; she blasted me with a scowl as she closed the heavy wooden door.

I sat among twenty empty desks and tapped my pencil in time with the red secondhand on the big classroom clock. *Tick, tick, tick, tick...*

I couldn't focus. I wrote numbers in without figuring them out.

Turning to the last page, I sighed. It had about a hundred problems on it. No way could I finish before lunch ended.

I quickly ripped it out and threw it in the garbage. *There.* Now I was free.

Wait. She'd see it there. I'd be in even worse trouble than I was now. She'd definitely tell my mom if I got caught. I opened the door to the hallway. Only a shiny tile floor and closed doors on both sides.

I pulled my wadded-up last page out of the trashcan. Mrs. Cross would probably come back soon. I needed to hurry and figure this out. *She wouldn't think to look outside, would she?*

I stepped out the other door onto the playground. A silver trash can sat in front of one of the outbuildings, so I tossed it in and scurried back to the classroom. Now she'd never know.

I placed my math packet, sans last page, on top of her stack of turned-in papers. *Where could Mrs. Cross be?*

I sat at my desk and waited. The red second hand made its orbit around the black-framed clock. Tick, tick, tick...

What if she notices this is the only packet without that last page? Could I say it must have gotten lost?

No, she'd never believe that. I opened the bottom file cabinet drawer, where she kept our assignments. I sorted through until I found the math packets like the one I'd just turned in. I pulled out the stack and proceeded to tear the last page off every one of them, piling them on the floor.

I replaced them in the file folder and closed the cabinet. With a quick glance at the hallway door, I slipped outside again with the pile of last pages, setting them on the side of the can. I took a deep breath and let them slide over, fluttering into the empty can.

Now all I had to do was wait.

I waited. And waited. And waited.

Mrs. Cross never remembered me that day. When I noticed my class playing outside, I finally decided to head down to the lunchroom on my own. I gulped down my lunch and made it back as class was starting again.

A few days later, I sat in my desk, swinging my legs and working math problems. I watched Mrs. Cross crouch in front of her file cabinet, pull out a file, and thumb through a stack of packets. "I am *sure* I put that page in here," she said. She looked through more packets before slamming the file cabinet shut and returning to her desk with a confused look on her face.

Later, she stood above my desk with a packet in hand. Her hair hung down and covered most of her face, except her frown.

I froze. How would I explain the pile of math pages in the garbage can? Why hadn't I hidden them better?

She set the packet down and showed me the last few pages. It looked like a red checkmark factory had exploded. "I want you to fix these." She turned on the heel of her sensible shoes and walked away.

I breathed a sigh of relief and pulled my worn pink eraser out of my desk. I was good at fixing stuff.

Chapter Five

So why couldn't I fix the hole in my heart? It was like the hole in the page of my children's book. No magical tape could fill it.

Was I doomed to this empty and lonely space for the rest of my life, feeling like that day in Mrs. Cross' class at lunch? No matter how hard I tried, I could not erase the memories that played like movie scenes, over and over.

I might have prevailed in the big argument Doug and I had about whether to go to small group, but he was right about my need to get outside of my four walls. I couldn't stay alone forever.

When I saw a church announcement for a new ladies' Bible study, I signed up. Weirsbe's study of Isaiah would be a challenge, but perhaps it would draw more women like me, who wanted to talk more about theology than fashion and home décor.

We squeezed around a knee-high Sunday school room table in chairs designed for elementary students. The room was painted burnt orange and smelled like dirty socks.

Each week after the study, I tried to start conversations as we made our way down the long church hallways, but more often than not, they were politely cut short.

Just keep trying, I told myself. Sometimes it takes awhile to get the friendship started.

Week after week, group discussion often turned to how

wonderful it was to be part of the church. I learned that each one of the Bible study attendees had been members since it started, friends for fifteen years. Clearly, I was the newbie, having only been a member for three years.

During one meeting, the discussion had gone down a rabbit trail and eventually led to the subject of introverts.

One outspoken lady said, "I don't think it's a personality thing. I just think introverts are selfish."

What?

She went on to explain that introverts keep to themselves because they don't want to give to others. I thought of all the times I'd trailed them down the hall, hoping to wedge a word or two into their conversations, maybe invite someone out to coffee. All the times I'd sat in small group listening to gregarious personalities. How drained gatherings left me.

I kept silent, but inside I stewed. *Extroverts are the selfish ones. They can talk over an introvert like a bulldozer without noticing it's a one-sided conversation.*

How could I relate to these ladies? After each meeting, I felt worse and worse. Was it the heaviness of the prophet Isaiah's words? Or was it feeling insignificant, like the outsider that I was? There was no shaking this cloud over me. Perhaps others sensed it and stayed away, like one stays inside during heavy rain showers.

The final straw came not long after. I sat next to an elderly lady, the pastor's mother-in-law. Across the table sat her good friend. When I spoke during discussion, I noticed them make eye contact. Their faces expressed annoyance.

What? Is it something I said? I tried again. Same effect. It happened a few times more, regardless of what I said, until I decided to stop talking. So, *not only am I insignificant, but apparently really irritating too.* During my drive home, I tried to figure out what it could have been that bothered them. I came up with nothing.

Maybe none of them wanted me there. Could they sense the secrets I kept? Did they somehow know that beneath my cheerful veneer, I wasn't the put-together Christian I appeared to be? I'd worked so hard not to let anyone see my brokenness.

I wondered, at what point do I give up on trying to foster relationships? It was so much easier to pretend to be connected to people through Facebook than to try to do real-life relationships. Lately, it took all of my energy just to get out the door.

I rode to church in silence a few weeks later. I'd been doing an experiment—would anyone talk to me if I didn't say "hi" first? Two weeks in a row, I hadn't said a word, and no one sought me out either. *I really am invisible*, I thought.

That day, the Bible study leader appeared in front of me as we sat in the sanctuary, waiting for the service to start. She grabbed both of my hands. "We've missed you at Bible study. Will you be coming back this week?"

I fought the urge to yank my hands away, and instead pulled away slowly and politely. "It's been pretty busy," I said. "Tuesday mornings probably aren't going to work for me."

The band started playing onstage. She looked at me with sympathy, made her regrets, and returned to her seat. That was weird, I thought. Maybe they really did want me there? I could have sworn they didn't.

Numbly, I sat through the service. I couldn't feel God there amidst the loud music and the song leader's chastising us for not worshiping vigorously enough. In my mind, I'd already made my way through the packed foyer to the safety of the car, away from throngs of happy, chatty people. Ironic how we can be loneliest in a crowd.

As we drove home, Doug left me to my thoughts.

What was the point of going to church? I didn't feel closer to God there. Maybe a relationship with Him was all an illusion. If He did care about what I was going through, I sure didn't see any signs. Had I ever known Him at all?

I'd been introduced to Him as a child. Was that experience much like other childhood experiences, like Santa Claus, or the Easter Bunny?

Easter Sunday, when I was eight, seven of us from Sunday school lined up in front of the pulpit, ready to recite the memory verses we'd rehearsed the day before. As I said mine, I held up a crown of thorns and kept my eyes on Joan, our teacher, watching for signs of approval, that I had done it right.

Others spotted their parents in the congregation, seated on gleaming wooden pews. I didn't bother to look. I knew mine wouldn't be there. Normally, I walked the five blocks from my house alone, occasionally accompanied by my little brother.

On any given Sunday morning, my dad would sit at the dining room table with a cup of coffee and the newspaper. Smoke swirled from a cigarette sitting in the ashtray overflowing with butts, and the Statler Brothers crooned a scratchy ballad over the LP player. After sitting on his lap and reading the "funnies" together, I would hop down and put on a dress for Sunday school.

In the basement of that church, I learned about Jesus, Moses, and Joseph. After a rousing rendition of "Father Abraham," our class would plop breathless into metal folding chairs to hear flannelgraph stories and create masterpieces out of cotton balls and Popsicle sticks.

On weekdays, I often went to hang out at the church with

Joan, the Sunday school teacher. One day, she caught me in another classroom, riffling through stickers and stashing some in my pockets. I could only stare, mouth agape.

She didn't say a word about my theft. "Come with me. I have a little project for you."

As we set about preparing crafts for next Sunday's lesson, taking the stickers began to get to me. I knew it was wrong. But why didn't she yell at me? Wasn't she going to tell me I was bad?

"Joan, what if we do a bad thing? Is Jesus mad?"

"I don't know about mad, but I think it makes Him sad."

"But how do we fix it? How can we make Jesus happy again?"

"Jesus will forgive us for everything if we ask Him." This was the first time I'd ever been convicted of a specific sin, instead of a general feeling of guilt and shame.

Soon after, during a Sunday morning lesson, Joan offered to pray with us if we wanted to ask Jesus to forgive us and wash us clean from our sins. Boy, did I ever! I prayed that prayer with my eyes squeezed shut and tried to make her words my own there in the basement.

The morning of my baptism was the only day I can ever remember my parents attending church together. While I put on my white robe backstage, Mom stood at the podium and sang "What a Friend We Have in Jesus."

Behind the stage, a tank of water served as the baptismal. Normally, red curtains covered the big window to the baptistery, but that day they hung open. I stepped into warm water, joining the pastor. He wore a white robe too.

While he spoke to the people through the window, I mentally rehearsed what I was supposed to do. Answer the question, cross my arms, and let the pastor cover my mouth and nose with a white cloth. I'd practiced dipping backwards in the tub earlier that week just so I knew I could do it.

He pulled a white cloth out of his pocket. "Lyneta, do you accept Jesus as your savior?"

I nodded, doe-eyed and completely forgetting what I was supposed to say. As he tipped me backward, I held my breath and shut my eyes tight as the water rushed over my face. Before I knew it, he was pulling me out again. I breathed a sigh of relief—it wasn't as bad as I thought.

Surprisingly, life didn't change any afterward. I'd hoped it would turn me into a different person, one who could keep from sinning. It was just as hard to be a good person as before.

I'd desperately wanted to gain God's acceptance. Though I'd had a little taste of the attention I craved from the people who congratulated me on my baptism, something deep down told me I still wasn't good enough.

Living a sin-free life became a full-time worry. I took long showers, hoping to scrub off any uncleanness I'd accrued by talking back to my parents or talking in class. I wracked my brain in bed each night, trying to think of stuff I'd done to confess at night before I slipped off to sleep.

What if I forgot to ask forgiveness for one thing and God couldn't let me into heaven? The thought of burning in hell forever and ever kept me awake long after Dad tucked me in.

I hadn't thought of hell in a long time, but my current life sure did resemble it.

At home that afternoon, I was washing Sunday dinner dishes when Doug wrapped his arms around me from behind and snuggled me for a long time. "It seems like we should find another church," he finally said.

I took a deep breath and dried my hands, then turned around to face him. "I'm sorry. I know you love it there."

"I'm sorry you don't." No arguments about whether I'm trying, no debates about hard it was for me to fit in. Just simple understanding.

"I really did try."

"I know."

I hugged him again, absorbing his warmth. It had been a long, cold winter. Spring didn't bring any promises of sunshine and blue skies, either.

I didn't know how much longer I could pretend a lifetime of secrets wasn't suffocating me. But the truth was becoming undeniable: secrets had always threatened my stability, for as long as I could remember.

"It's a secret. You have to promise to never tell." My friend, Lana, lay beside me in the back yard where we'd spread old quilts on the grass. It was only us two and about a million stars overhead.

"Of course." I hadn't seen her since she'd moved to Arkansas a couple years ago, but at thirteen, we still spent every waking and sleeping moment together whenever we saw each other, like we'd always done.

"Not anyone. Ever."

I rolled over on my side to face her. "I won't tell. Now spill it."

She had just spent a few weeks with her dad, stepmom, and teenage stepbrother, Cody.

"Cody makes me touch *his thing*."

Gross. "What? Why?"

"He calls it Mr. Happy. Mr. Happy likes it when I touch it."

I shuddered at the thought of the boy I'd met a few times doing that to my friend. She was three years younger than me. "Why don't you tell your mom?"

"Because, Cody will get into a lot of trouble. What if I didn't get to go visit my dad anymore?"

I hadn't thought of that. She was right. Telling the secret would be really bad. As the summer evening grew chilly, we pulled one of the quilts up to our chins and settled in for sleep.

If there was anything I knew to be true, it was that a kid's family circumstances could be upside down without notice. Families were unpredictable enough without stirring things up.

Late in my third-grade year, I walked the block or so from our elementary school to the babysitter's house where my brother stayed after kindergarten. From there, he and I walked up four more blocks to our house, where we'd usually grab a snack and plop down in front of our black-and-white TV to watch *Electric Company* and *Reading Rainbow*.

Except the living room was empty when we opened the door. The TV wasn't there. Neither were the dining room table or chairs. A plywood board covered the space where the couch had been. The only thing left was the stereo system.

We ran to each room, hoping to find a clue. My bed was missing, but we found my brother's in his bedroom. Our parents' bedroom still looked the same.

Where could it all have gone? Surely, when Mom and Dad got home from work, they'd tell us. We weren't sure what to do since there wasn't a television to watch.

Around dinnertime, we pelted Dad with questions the minute he walked in the door. "Hey, where's all the furniture?" "Why isn't Mom home?"

He looked around as if he expected the furniture to still be there. "I don't know."

We followed him through the house as he inspected each room, just as we had.

We peppered him with more questions, but the more we asked, the more drawn his face became. "Can't you see that I don't know any more than you do? Go outside until I call you for dinner."

We reluctantly obeyed.

Later that night, the house was eerily quiet without TV. As we ate around a card table, I asked Dad when Mom was going to come home.

He put his fork down and looked me in the eye. "I don't know."

"Were you talking to her on the phone?"

"Yeah." His face tinged with pain.

"Where is she?"

"At Jan's house." He picked up his fork and started to eat again.

Apparently, that was all the information I could pry out of him. I didn't need to ask why she would go stay with her best friend, who lived a few miles away.

She was moving out and they were splitting up.

Should I be worried? We'd been through this before, and they got back together. I decided not to tell anyone at school. What would my classmates think about my broken family? Their parents were all still married.

A few days later, Mom took us to stay in her one-bedroom apartment. My brother and I shared the double bed, while she slept on the couch.

I begged her to let us stay at Dad's in our old bedrooms during the week, but she only let us on the weekends.

Shortly before school let out, Mom, Dad, Monte, and I spent an awkward evening at the park together.

Mom noticed me sulking while Dad pushed Monte on the merry-go-round. "What's wrong with you?" I should have known the tone in her voice was a warning, not an invitation to share my feelings.

I shrugged. "I just wish you and Dad weren't splitting up."

"Well, you could just enjoy a trip to the park right now. I thought you'd want to do something fun."

And just pretend nothing's wrong?

My chest squeezed, crushed by sadness. I started to cry. "I wouldn't be so sad if you hadn't left!"

Mom grabbed me by the arm and pulled me into the car. "If you keep trying to get us back together, I'm going to move you far, far away from your dad and you won't see him anymore. Do you understand me?"

I nodded, hoping she'd release her painful grip. *No! We can't move away!* I couldn't be without my daddy!

When she let go, I blinked back my tears and sucked in a deep breath. I hadn't even considered the possibility of moving to another town. Even though I wanted to have fun with my daddy, I was relieved when we left the park after that. Clearly, my true feelings weren't safe to share.

From then on, whenever I felt sadness or hurt about the breakup, I did my best to push it aside. Maybe if I were good enough, I could keep things from getting worse.

For the rest of the school year, we shuffled back and forth between Mom's apartment and Dad's house. I didn't tell my classmates about our new living arrangement.

Mom dropped us off at Dad's house one night. He was sitting on a new-to-us floral green couch. He'd also bought a console Technicolor TV and a used dinette. Juice Newton's "Just Call Me Angel" played on the radio. Monte and I went around the room, exclaiming our approval for each new piece of furniture.

"So, since you have a TV now, is it okay if I take the stereo?" Mom stood by the front door as if to make a hasty exit.

"No, it's not *okay*." Dad glanced up at her, but returned his attention to the book on his lap.

"Why not?"

They argued for a few minutes, getting louder and louder.

Finally, Mom flung open the screen door. "Fine." She called dad a vulgar name as the door slammed behind her.

Just keep quiet and don't make waves, I kept telling myself. Then everything will be okay.

But it wasn't okay. Not then, and it certainly didn't become okay by stuffing my feelings about the mistreatment I'd received for the last three decades. The flashbacks were not going to go away.

I thought of calling Lana. But would that help? Why, oh, why did I keep that secret for her? I wondered whether she was going through the same thing right now as me.

Her situation could have gotten worse for all I knew, and she might not have been able to tell me. Did she ever think about it? I picked up my phone and found her number in my contacts.

I held my thumb over the "call" icon. What was I going to

say? If she had forgotten all about it and lived a happy life with her husband and three daughters, like in her Facebook posts, I would unnecessarily wreck a peaceful time in her life.

I don't want to be in a world where God allows girls to be hurt like that. Why didn't He protect me? Why didn't he protect Lana from her stepbrother?

I set the phone down. Who could I talk to? There wasn't one person who'd understand.

I was alone and invisible. I needed a miracle.

Chapter Six

2006-Newport, Oregon

"He's a miracle man, miracle man. No one can do...the things that he can."

One Easter Sunday at our Newport church, Jerusalem residents in homemade ancient Israel costumes milled across the stage, singing and waving palm leaves. Oh, to get a glimpse of the Miracle Man!

We'd been all smiles as Jesus crossed from stage right through the crowd. We reached out our hands, hoping for a touch from the Rabbi. Some of us played characters with serious physical defects—blindness, a withered arm, deafness—and Jesus stopped to heal them all.

During the last verse, a sorrowful man walked onto the stage with outstretched arms, carrying my youngest daughter, sprawled out with her head hanging back and arms splayed out. She lay lifeless.

I marveled at her ability to be perfectly still, because in real life she was either at 90 MPH or asleep. But even that time during practice when her grieving "dad" accidentally knocked her head against the wall as he moved onstage, she stayed in character as the little dead girl.

The man handed her to Jesus, who lifted her heavenward, closed his eyes, and moved his lips in prayer. The way his arms shook, I could tell it was the last year she'd be able to play a little girl. She was getting too big.

Suddenly, the limp girl bolted upright with a smile that lit up the stage. After hugging Jesus, she jumped down to hug her jubilant father.

As part of the crowd, I pasted an amazed and excited look on my face. I tried to contain an amused smile. The man who played the father didn't care for hugs; the little girl gave them lavishly.

As the song ended on a dramatic note, we clapped and shouted, "Hosanna!"

A few minutes later, we stood on the same stage, surrounding the same Jesus, with fists raised. "Crucify him! His blood be on us and our children!"

Roman soldiers banged a hammer on a metal spike next to the cross near Jesus' hands and the sound reverberated throughout the sanctuary. Jesus remembered to cry out in pain.

"I'm pretty sure that hurt," Pastor Mark, our director, had said during dress rehearsal, giving last-minute directions to make the scene more realistic.

I clinched my fists as Roman soldiers raised Jesus up. He was gripping the invisible wires around the crossbeam as tightly as he could. Those and only a small board to stand on held him on the cross. I mentally willed him to stay up there. He was a last-minute addition to the cast, covering for the actor originally playing Jesus, who fell during practice and sprained his ankle.

Thankfully, we got through the rest of the crucifixion scene and burial without any injuries, and on Easter morning, as usual, the Son rose triumphantly at dawn. A happy crowd sang "Hosanna, Hosanna," as Jesus ascended into the clouds.

I recalled the joy at pulling off another successful cantata and then packing up the paper *mâché* tomb and stone, and putting away the rigging used to hoist Jesus into the air. Next week, the workers would come and patch the hole in the sanctuary wall where Jesus crawled out into the back hallway between the burial and resurrection. And all the hard work was worth it for a little bit of magic to believe in.

People I didn't recognize would come up and speak to me like they'd known me forever. Shows were hard work, but all of that effort had helped build the façade. I was visible, more visible than most. I was significant, an insider in the church. My position as worship pastor's assistant meant that I was "on staff." By grit, and with very little grace, I had overcome a traumatic childhood, domestic violence, and a divorce, and I'd created the role I wanted in the perfect Christian life.

I'd learned this much as Doug and I rebuilt our lives from the ashes: In the real world, there was no magic. But I'd left all of that behind when we moved from Newport, and now I was back to being unseen and irrelevant.

If I wanted to be seen, if I wanted to be worthy of love, I needed to do something significant. Churches with choirs were almost extinct. Given the musical talent around Nashville, I wasn't needed in music ministry.

I quickly thought of my devotional book. *Of course!* Before I made the decision to go back to college and finish my degree, I had started writing a devotional. Why not revise it and shop it around to publishers? Though I hadn't worked on any other writing except academia since starting classes, I decided to brush off the manuscript and register for a writing clinic in Nashville.

A few weeks later, I arrived as unprepared as I'd ever been for anything. I had downloaded everyone else's material, but hadn't made a single mark on any of them. All weekend long, I faked my way through each critique session, managing to be encouraging and affirming while repeating others' constructive remarks.

The last night, the nine of us hopeful writers dined together on fried alligator tail and catfish with our mentor amidst a background of bluegrass music.

I asked him how to beef up the marketing section on my proposal, since I had no blog and fewer than a thousand Facebook friends.

"If you really want to promote your writing," he told me, "You have to speak regularly."

Get up in front of people and speak? About what?

"I can put on a red curly wig and sing and dance as Mrs. Paroo, but I wouldn't ever be comfortable being up there as *me*," I said. "I love performing, but—"

"It's still a performance," he said. "You're just portraying the self you want to show your audience."

I thought about that. Was there any part of me worth showing an audience? No, I would have to find another way to market this book. I was here to write, not speak.

I went back home with a plan to polish up my proposal and pitch it at a major writers conference the next month. In the meantime, I'd still have all my usual work to do, which was good because I'd have to knuckle down and ignore the memories to get it all done before May.

My phone's vibration interrupted, so I picked it up and clicked the decline button. I was on the clock—whoever it was would have to wait until later.

Wait... It was Patti. I called her back.

"Well, how *are* you?" She was anticipating hearing my

excitement about finishing school and heading to Oregon for graduation.

I started, but couldn't bring myself to say, "fine." Not to Patti.

"Well, I really *should be* fine."

A pause. "Uh oh. But you're not?"

"I'm going through a little bit of a rough spot."

Normally, I'd be scared to admit I wasn't doing fantastic. Instead, I was relieved.

I didn't go into details—how could I share the horrific scenes I'd been reliving in my brain? I couldn't let even Patti see the reality beyond my stage-perfect front.

When we met over a decade ago, she said, "God gave you some spunk for a reason."

I didn't feel like I had any spunk left, but talking with her again was like salve on a wound. She shared some recent struggles of her own that made her feel overcome with sadness—at least she understood what it was like for a strong, independent woman to feel so overwhelmed and weak. After promising to pray for me, she reminded me that I had a forever friend across the miles and said goodbye.

I sat at my desk with the cursor blinking in my Word document for a long time. I wasn't that scared, helpless little girl anymore, but I clung to her words like a terrified toddler clings to a nurturing parent.

During childhood, I didn't have many moments where I felt important to the adults in my life, but one memory stood out.

I let the wind blow through my hair, riding across town in the passenger seat of my Aunt Beckie's red VW bug. She was my mom's younger sister, in the midst of a divorce of her own. My cousin, a toddler named Willie, wasn't with us, but my brother sat in the back seat. We whizzed down Main Street in Sheridan with the windows down and Juice Newton's "Queen of Hearts" blaring.

We were headed to Kmart. It was the summer before fourth grade, and Mom had recently moved from her apartment in Buffalo to another apartment in Sheridan, thirty miles away.

Beckie's carefree personality matched her curly, unruly black hair. When I was with her, I felt free to talk and share my feelings. She listened to me and it seemed like she genuinely cared.

I could hardly believe I'd overheard Beckie telling Mom she wanted to buy us all new school clothes. Usually when we got a new outfit, it was for our birthday or Christmas. Mostly we wore hand-me-downs. But a whole bunch of new clothes at once?

When we arrived at the store, Beckie let us pick out several brand-new outfits.

"Look at this one! You should get it." I held up a yellow and burgundy striped long-sleeved shirt with a collar and waved it at my brother.

Monte scrunched his face and shook his head no.

Beckie helped us find our sizes and suggested some outfits. I especially loved my new burgundy, cotton print dress and brown clogs.

Times with Aunt Beckie were a fun escape from reality. We went lots of places "just us." We saw *Superman III* and went out for dessert at Perkins. Sometimes we spent the night in her cabin, where we'd help cook dinner and wash dishes by hand before bedding down on the floor. She didn't say so in as many words, but I knew she understood and wanted to cheer us up.

The cabin, a small one-bedroom with logs painted red, stood out in the country underneath tall pine trees. It had been in our family for as long as I could remember; my great-grandparents had lived there before they sold it to Beckie.

Mom's new apartment in Sheridan was bigger than the one-bedroom in Buffalo, but my brother and I still shared a bedroom. I spent the long, hot days wishing to play with old friends and see Dad. Two weeks between our visits to Buffalo dragged on and on.

Unlike at Dad's house, there were no books, no Rubik's cube, and no cable TV. When Mom was home, she pushed us outside to play with other kids from the apartment complex. I had no idea how to make friends with strangers; I only wanted to be with the ones I'd known from Kindergarten.

It still wasn't safe to express any feelings to Mom, even when she demanded to know them. "What's wrong with you? Why are you moping?"

I couldn't get out of answering a direct question, so I decided to keep it simple. "I miss my Dad."

I could tell by her downturned lips that it was the wrong answer. "Well, do you cry about missing me when you're at your dad's house?"

"No," I answered honestly. Usually the short two-night stay whizzed by too fast to miss her.

She huffed and then turned away in disgust. Most times, she was either ignoring me or getting on my case. I counted the days until the next weekend with Dad.

At summer's end, I began fourth grade in a new school where I didn't know a soul. As the days turned cooler, I spent recesses alone on the playground and counted the hours until

I could be back home. Such as it was.

Whenever I rode in the backseat, I memorized landmarks in my new town, thinking if Mom got really mad and left me somewhere I needed to know how to get back to her place. I didn't think about what I'd do then.

I lived for Dad's weekends when I could be back at our old house and see my friends in the neighborhood.

One early Sunday morning shortly after school started, I was awoken by a phone call.

"Hello?" Dad answered. His deep voice rang through the house.

A long silence followed. *Who could be calling this early?*

"I'm sorry to hear that."

Curious, I got out of bed and wandered to the couch to hear, but Dad stretched the long, curly cord back into his bedroom. I could only make out muffled tones.

In a few minutes, he came back out to the living room and hung it up.

"Who was it, Dad?"

"It was your mom." He plunked down on a dining room chair and lit a cigarette. His face looked sad.

That can't be good. "What did she say?"

He stared at the table, his thoughts far away.

"Dad. What did she say?"

"It's your Grandpa Darwin. He had a heart attack yesterday." Dad looked me in the eye and swallowed hard. "He's passed away."

"No!" I jumped up and ran into my bedroom, throwing myself onto the unmade bed. I cried long and hard. We'd stayed at my grandparents' house for weeks at a time during summers. He'd taken us fishing, arrowhead hunting, and to church. I couldn't hear a hymn without thinking about his big, booming voice belting out the melody.

Could that tall, larger-than-life man, the one who always wore the "Wyoming Game and Fish" badge on his red shirts really be gone? They had only retired a few years ago and moved from Pinedale to a big place in the Black Hills.

After awhile, I dried my tears and put on some church clothes. No morning comics or snuggles with Dad today—I had to get to church.

When I went back into the living room, Dad had gotten dressed and taken the newspaper to his normal Sunday morning spot at the dining room table. "Your mom's coming to pick you up later."

Without asking my brother if he wanted to go, I headed for the front door. "I'll be back after church." I closed the big door carefully and then ran the five blocks to church. Way early for class, I found no one in the Sunday school rooms downstairs, so I followed organ music upstairs. Two ladies who'd been my teachers, Joan and Jeannie, practiced the morning's service hymns in the sanctuary. I coasted down the aisle in a daze.

"Are you okay?" Joan stepped off the platform and came to give me a hug.

"My grandpa died."

They looked at each other with wide eyes.

"Oh, I thought it might be something like that," Joan said.

Jeannie followed her off the platform and they invited me to sit with them on the front pew, stroking my back and telling me how sorry they were. Sunday school and church service went by in a blur.

After church, I slow-stepped home along my familiar route, pondering all of the changes swirling like the cottonwood leaves in the autumn breeze above me.

I couldn't fathom a life without my Grandpa. To me, he was a giant of a man, both physically and in personality. He stood over six feet tall and wore a cowboy hat. In my eyes, he could have bench-pressed his orange Ford pickup.

When Mom came to pick us up, my neighbor friend, Mindy, pressed her face against the screen door. "Can you play?"

I wanted to so badly, but I shook my head no and sadly waved goodbye. We trudged to the car.

I wore my new dress from Kmart to the graveside service. Mom told my brother and I to go over to our dad, who stood off to the side and away from the family at the coffin. It was unusually warm for September that year. The sunshine, long green grass, and blue sky betrayed the cold, dark inside me. Not even God cared how I felt.

Grandpa Darwin was with God, but they were also going to bury him in the ground. I imagined being stuck inside the tiny coffin surrounded by dirt. In my imagination, I was pounding on the lid from inside, screaming to be let out. My heart started pounding and I got dizzy standing next to my dad.

I tried to sit on the grass but a thistle sticker jabbed me through my tights and I shot up again woozily, and grabbed my dad's arm. He was listening to the pastor and put his arm around me absently.

After the soloist, the service ended, and people filed back to their cars. I recognized Joan, my Sunday school teacher, walking toward me.

"I've been meaning to get this to you. It's been sitting in the church office for awhile." She handed me an envelope and moved away toward the throng of people leaving the graveyard.

"Thank you." I opened it to find a certificate of baptism with my name in big letters across the front.

It seemed so long ago: before my parents' marriage exploded, before our family ripped apart, before I lost my Grandpa. Life was more secure then, though still scary at times. But now? I knew the world could turn upside down in a moment. What could I trust? Who could I talk to?

I took the certificate home and tucked it into my Bible.

I agreed to return with Doug to Aaron's office for another round of counseling. Most of the hour centered on me, so it was clear we weren't there for marriage counseling. Doug was only there to make sure I was. I wanted to explain enough to improve our relationship, but not enough to reveal my secret, which felt far too dirty to reveal.

"I keep remembering things from my childhood and when I was a teenager. I can't keep the memories from coming, and they're terrifying. I know they happened a long time ago, but it's like they're happening right now."

"It sounds like PTSD," Aaron said. "Shutting down was your mind's way of protecting you from what you couldn't handle when you were younger."

His diagnosis made sense. It did feel a little bit like I was in a war zone. I left the office that day with a better understanding of what was going on. But it didn't give me any greater coping strategies.

When I explained to the girls, I noticed a change in the way they treated me. Instead of their usual teenage resistance, they spoke to me as if I'd break. They often asked if they could do something to help me, which was quite a switch from my previous taskmaster approach to getting them to do their chores.

Though I appreciated their concern, it worried me. Did they know how deep into the pit I'd gone? Could they see I was only pretending to be the strong, confident Mom? I was staggering under the weight of all the secrets, but I feared losing either their trust or their good opinion forever if I shared with them.

And with Doug, would he think I was damaged beyond repair too? I could imagine him reeling with the thought that I'd become tainted by what was done to me. I felt ruined for good. How could I ever have a normal relationship?

No, this was something I had to deal with myself, no matter what. If we could find a church where I could fit in, maybe I could start serving again and be more like my old self. After I graduated, I'd have that degree and prove I was fine and capable with a new career after Katie graduated high school.

My only challenge—find out how to do that while it felt like I was plodding through wet cement.

One morning, while looking for one of my literature texts for school, I came across the book on sexual abuse in the pile I'd ordered from Amazon. Forgetting my task, I cozied up with it on the couch. As I read page after page, it was as though the author's voice spoke only to me.

Then I came across something that stunned me. She asked why so many suffered in silence, dealing with horrible memories all by themselves.

I hadn't thought of that. *There were others out there like me?*

I felt a strange relief that I wasn't alone. Not that I was glad such horrible things had happened to others, but somehow my suffering lessened, knowing I wasn't the only one.

Some of them, like the author, had found healing. Was it possible for me? Was there a way to make the memories go away? I didn't know, but by some miracle I hoped so.

Chapter Seven

After the bully in the basement, I was defenseless, marked for anyone to take advantage of, especially in 1981 after Mom moved us to Sheridan.

Soon she met a rotund, balding man who played guitar and owned a construction company. They began spending every evening together. I overheard my mom tell someone on the phone that he reminded her of Kenny Rogers. He did have the round belly, grey hair, and beard. I'd heard all the Kenny Rogers LPs. They were Mom's favorite.

They liked to stand together hugging a lot. Seeing this virtual stranger so affectionate with my mom didn't feel right. Though I was ten, I'd wriggle between them and look up at their faces, looking down at me.

"I think something's come between us," Kenny would say with a smirk.

He had already been married three times and had lots of kids and step-kids. Most of them were adults. When we visited his place, it was a little like crashing a frat party. I hadn't ever seen a music video before, but I soon had the current rotation memorized, since MTV blared at all hours.

Soon, Mom and Kenny were planning a December wedding.

During Christmas break, Mom, my brother Monte, and I moved across town to Kenny's property. He'd built two houses and set up two trailer houses on a few acres. Our small, simple household expanded to several of Kenny's adult sons and a tenant family on the lot. Everything shifted again—new rules, new school (because we were in a different district), new church. We started attending Kenny's church as a family every Sunday, where he sang in the choir.

Kenny and Mom traveled a lot the first few months they were married. My brother and I often stayed with a family who lived up the hill from us. They had three boys. The youngest and I were both in fourth grade, but we had different teachers. The middle one was a couple grades ahead of us, and the oldest went to middle school.

One weekend while we were staying with them, my brother and I were hanging out with them in their big family room in the basement. The oldest one barricaded the door with a reclining chair and then sat in it.

I pleaded with him to let me out of the room for several minutes, to no avail. I didn't want to be trapped in the basement with a bunch of boys!

"Sit in my lap real quick, and then you can leave." He leaned back in the chair, and laced his fingers together behind his head.

I stood in front of him, hands on hips. "Let. Me. Out."

He laughed.

I tried to shove the recliner away from the door. "Now!"

He grabbed my arm. I spun around to walk away, but he pulled me down onto his lap.

He squeezed me around the waist, and every time I squirmed, he'd say, "Ahh, that feels good." He must have held me there for a whole minute. A minute that stretched into an eternity.

Finally, I landed a blow to his rib with my elbow.

He yelped and let go long enough for me to escape.

I backed away from him. Eventually, he moved the chair so I could go upstairs.

I managed to avoid him the rest of the weekend, but I wouldn't be able to avoid him forever.

Mom hired him to babysit my brother and me some evenings. I hadn't told about the time in the basement, but after a scary episode where he exposed himself to me after my brother had gone to bed, I finally told my mom all the stuff that had been going on.

"Okay, I'll take care of it." Mom left it at that.

I breathed a sigh of relief, knowing that at least I wouldn't have to fear being around him anymore. Navigating a new school and neighborhood, not to mention the every-other-weekend only schedule with my dad, was hard enough as it was.

While walking home from the bus stop a few days later, I saw the bawdy babysitter. "You won't be babysitting me anymore," I said, my voice sing-songy and taunting. "I told my mom what you did and now she's mad at you."

He only said, "So?"

Back in our house, I mentioned to Mom that I'd already told him she was going to fire him.

"I wish you hadn't said anything. Now you probably hurt his feelings."

If she ever did say anything to him after that, I never found out about it. Thankfully, at the end of the school year, Kenny's renters moved to another state. The four of us moved from my stepbrothers' house to the recently vacated house up the hill.

I made another new discovery on the back of the toilet tank—glossy magazines with pictures of naked ladies. Curious, I read story after story of bizarre sex acts. Was that normal? People really did that stuff to each other? Given Mom's tendency to brush away any of my concerns, I knew not to mention it. Talking about things before had not gone over well before, so I tucked my guilty curiosity away and added it to my secrets, burying my many questions.

It was one of many ways I navigated my new scary world without guidance. Another was Kenny's confusing affection. He was different than my dad, who'd mostly let me initiate hugs or crawl up into his lap. Kenny's assertive manner confused me. On one hand, I craved a daddy's attention. On the other hand, he wasn't *my* dad; I felt a little disloyal. Plus, I wasn't altogether sure about the flip-flop my belly did sometimes when Kenny showed affection.

The first time it happened, he was tucking my brother and I in, like Dad did. At first, Monte and I shared a room and slept in a bunk bed. Instead of a fatherly kiss on the forehead, he gave me an open-mouth kiss on the neck.

I looked up at him in surprise. Obviously enjoying my reaction, he winked and grinned, then went out the door.

I lay there trying to understand what just happened. It was just a fatherly goodnight kiss, right? Still, the feeling that something wasn't quite right niggled at my brain. But nothing had happened nearly as bad as what the bully and the teenage babysitter had done, so I shrugged it off. Even if I had been able to express my feelings, who would listen?

At the same time, I became increasingly alarmed about my developing body. Whether or not anyone else noticed, I hoped I wouldn't change too quickly. I'd examine myself in the bathroom mirror and pray that any development wasn't as noticeable as it seemed to me.

None of the other girls in my fifth-grade class showed signs of needing to wear a bra. I tried to wear the loosest shirts I had, at least to school. I worried my changing body would only attract more attention. It terrified me so I hated it.

Early in the school year, Mom brought a K-Mart bag into my bedroom. "I bought you some training bras. You need to start wearing them."

Oh, no! It was noticeable! I panicked. "No! I don't want to wear them."

She slapped me across the face. "Yes, you will! If I catch you not wearing them, I'm going to spank you with the belt!" Her voice raised like it often did these days, but the threat of a belt meant it'd be an especially heinous offense. Why, I had no idea.

I held my cheek with one hand and took the bag with the other. I sucked in a deep breath and willed myself not to cry.

She left the room, still breathing heavily. The door closed with a thud.

My cheek still smarting, I slowly cut off the tags and put one on, a prisoner resigned to her fate.

I thought of the girls at school. It was hard enough to fit in with my bushy hair and chipped teeth. Now I'd be even more of a freak.

The first week, my worst fears came to pass. One of the girls passed by at the back of the classroom as I hung up my jacket. "Are you wearing a bra?" she sneered.

I glowered. "None of your business."

"You are." The glee in her voice drew attention from other classmates. Even boys, to my horror. I ignored their comments and waited it out until they grew bored and found something else to make fun of. I never did make many friends in that class and I couldn't wait for the school year to end.

In the summer before sixth grade, Mom and Kenny announced that we were moving over the mountain to a tiny town I'd never heard of called Otto, WY. A population of 50, the town was so isolated, it would take an hour on the bus to get to the nearest public school.

Needless to say, most times it was just the four of us, except when Kenny's younger girls came for a visit. Few other friends or family ever visited. Since we rode the school bus, even extracurricular activities were out of the question, since that would mean having to get a ride home. But there was plenty of work to while away the time.

We lived in a nine-bedroom farmhouse Kenny and his sons had built for his former wife and their big family. The giant barn loft was full of hay and dust that made my eyes swell every time I went up there. Every morning and evening, we poured grain into troughs for the sheep and goats, and dump scraps into the pig trough, too afraid to get in the pen. When it froze, we had to take a crowbar to break the layer of ice over the water troughs so they could get a drink. In the afternoons, we gathered eggs, and when some of the chickens started laying in the loft, we took turns climbing the ladder to collect. With one fireplace and two small wood stoves in the basement and master bedroom, it got very cold in the winter. That meant many hours of hauling, cutting, and stacking wood. The stoves and fireplace burned from sunup to sundown, and long evenings were spent under quilts and electric blankets.

I turned to books as friends. If I couldn't have meaningful conversations, at least I could read about them and get to know the characters. I devoured the *Little House* series and *Chronicles of Narnia*, along with all the Judy Bloom books.

The cold and my longing for the affection of a daddy conspired to make me seek out Kenny's lap with my crocheting or embroidery project, whiling away the hours until bedtime, since we could only get two channels on television way out in the country.

One cold evening, Kenny started tracing up my inner thigh.

I pushed his hand away. "Don't."

"Why not? Don't you like it?"

I did but I didn't. And I knew it was wrong of him. But afraid I'd somehow asked for it, I played it off and brought up something else.

Around that time, an old girlfriend of Kenny's stopped by for an afternoon visit. Mom wasn't home, and they sat knee to knee at the dining room table, laughing and talking. After that, he became more insistent about where he put his hands when I sat on his lap. And when I resisted, he grew impatient with me.

I recall the evening I'd finally had enough.

I pushed his hand away and forced myself off. He scowled at me from his easy chair.

"What? Come back here."

"If you don't quit, I'm going to tell Mom." I walked to the couch and plopped down with my embroidery hoop and thread.

"Tell me what?" Mom called, quilting in the other room.

"Nothing." I narrowed my eyes at Kenny.

The next night, I passed by his chair to join Mom on the couch.

"Sit on my lap," he said. It sounded like an ordinary invitation, father to daughter. But I knew it wasn't.

"No." I sat next to Mom and unfolded my embroidery.

"*Yes.*" His voice carried a sharper-than-usual edge.

Mom and I both looked up in surprise at his insistence. "She doesn't have to if she doesn't want to," Mom said, much to my relief.

After that, he never asked again.

There were lots of behind closed-door discussions loud enough to hear. They mostly argued about the woman who came to visit and about money.

Soon after, Kenny told Mom he wanted a divorce. This time, I wasn't surprised—I'd seen it coming. But when they announced it, I lashed out at him—more for the abuse than the divorce, though I didn't realize it.

"Hey!" my mom said. "We both made the decision."

I stopped. I knew it was a lie. I'd heard them—it was all his decision.

From that point on, I said nothing. Hadn't I learned over and over that my feelings were unimportant? I pretended everything was fine. I knew from experience things wouldn't be great financially, but I was glad to be moving back close enough to see Dad regularly.

Dad had remarried and we had a step-sister I hadn't met, so I was excited. Mom, Monte, and I moved back to Sheridan on Kenny's property, but instead of the big house on the hill, we moved to a rusted-out trailer at the bottom of the lot. One of his stepsons had moved his family into the house where we lived before. We didn't have much contact with Kenny's adult kids, who lived in the other buildings, which made living there a little awkward. After Kenny visited us a time or two, I never heard from or spoke to him again.

Since Mom had gone back to work as a nurse's aid, Monte and I spent a lot of time alone in the rusted-out trailer. I was now in seventh grade, switched schools again to the middle school, but knew few of the other students and they'd been snotty to me. We weren't allowed extracurricular activities, because we had no ride and no money for extras.

With no friends, I whiled away the lonely hours with my familiar books, thankful the school library had a large selection.

Even now, as an adult, I could escape into a book whenever I wanted. School gave me lots of opportunities, and so did Amazon Prime. But God used the thing He knew I'd trust, a book, to open me up for rescue.

After reading the book about sexual abuse, I wondered why God allowed some girls to become targets. If one in every four girls had been sexually molested by the time they were eight, and even more by eighteen, I wondered was I just one of those not worth saving?

The only way to keep from thinking about it was to work harder. I prepared my book proposal to take to the writers conference, working, and writing my school assignments. All of my professors remarked at what a hard worker I was. I fell asleep with a book in my hands every night.

Anxiety over my crumbling identity ambushed me while driving or in the shower, the only places I couldn't distract myself. I didn't want to be that girl—I wasn't her anymore—the one who'd been abused and neglected. It seemed everyone I knew had a happy, healthy childhood. Or if they hadn't, they got over it. What was wrong with me?

Finally, on a beautiful spring morning in May, I made a trip to a bigger grocery store about thirty minutes away. On the way home, I thought about my life and my future. I was terrified that after graduation, I'd have to come out of my fast-paced, performance-driven world. I knew how to feel good by getting good grades, but could I succeed at writing and speaking as a career?

I pulled into the garage and turned off the engine. As the door went down, even the thought of unloading and putting away the groceries in the trunk exhausted me. How was I going to produce something worth people buying and reading and believe in it enough to talk about? I thought how nice it would be if I could just fall asleep one night and not wake up.

I pushed it away with a little stab of guilt for even thinking such a thing.

But it was tempting. And I was so tired. It could all be over, all this struggle and useless effort to feel okay and look the part.

Tears sprang to my eyes. "God, why did you even make me? What am I good for?" Tears flowed freely as I slumped over the steering wheel.

Then, out of nowhere, a voice spoke.

"Will you trust me with your story?"

I adjusted the rearview mirror to check the backseat. Empty.

Where had it come from? It wasn't audible, was it? But I'd heard it loud and clear.

"Excuse me?" I said.

Trust me with your story. I'll show you how I'll redeem it.

I wiped my eyes as peace warmed my body. The voice didn't sound like any I'd been hearing, the ones saying I was worthless. Too broken. A waste. The question came without shame or condemnation. It was a simple invitation.

It was God. It had to be, right? He answered me!

But what did it mean "trust Him with my story?"

And if I said no, what would happen? Would I stay miserable forever?

What else can I do?

But if I said yes, what would that mean?

In my mind, I saw a distraught heroine facing the final curtain of Act One. She stood on stage in my costume. What I'd once thought beautiful set pieces now revealed bare plywood and two-by-fours on the back side. As the hot lights dimmed, I realized everything I'd built as my security to be seen by others—a healthy marriage, homeschooled kids, good parenting, church leadership—it was only to mask a lonely, fearful little girl, desperate to prevent anyone knowing how ruined she was on the inside. No amount of costuming or makeup could conceal her false smile. Everything onstage amounted to little more than an attempt to make things appear fine. But they were not fine.

And now God was calling for a divine intermission. He'd offered to interrupt my performance to reset the stage. Could he rescue me from the lines I couldn't stop hearing, the ones that told me I wasn't loveable? Could he really redeem me and give me the abundant life I longed for?

How could he? I had no idea. And I was pretty sure I wasn't ready to face the person I really was behind the character I'd projected. But anything had to be better than hiding in the darkness, in this perfect spotlight I'd staged for myself.

"Okay," I said aloud, "I will. I'll trust you."

I gathered my purse from the passenger seat, fetched the grocery bags from the trunk, and carried it all into the house. I didn't know when or how He would rescue me, but for the first time in months, a tiny hope sparked.

Though on the outside, I still charged headlong into school assignments and my job, I was eager to see what my new role would be. I still had to work hard to make my goal of *summa cum laude* in a few short weeks.

But in the meantime, I kept mulling over my new secret. God Himself had seen me flailing in my harsh shadow-light and had spoken to me. Not just in a verse Bible verse or a phrase striking me a certain way, or in sage words from a wise Christian friend.

This was an actual message he'd meant just for me. And that small hope was everything. I was *someone*.

Chapter Eight

June 2014—Oregon State University

It's almost my turn! I sat among rows and rows of black gown-clad graduates. After three hours of lining up, marching across campus, and listening to speeches, I was eager to file up the grassy aisle at OSU's Reser Stadium to grab my diploma.

On my right, a college-age blonde texted with perfectly French-manicured nails about getting "hammered tonight." She wore pristine white Keds.

On my left, another early-20-something with dark curly hair and wrinkled gown reeked of whiskey. He texted too—unpunctuated versions of the question "Where's the party at?" to several of his friends. I'd overheard him say he couldn't wait to get the ceremony over with so he could get back to his drinking.

What am I doing here? I didn't know a soul, except for Doug and the girls in the stands. I couldn't even text them. I'd given Doug my phone for safekeeping as I'd gone to line up, thinking I'd need to be hands free as I walked across the stage.

I turned back to look at the covered bleachers. Hordes and hordes of people milled around, greeting graduates who already walked across the stage. I squinted to see if I could find Doug and the girls up there somewhere, but didn't spot them.

Another wave of sleepiness hit. Tonight, we'd all be together in Patti and Mark's beach house in Gleneden. It would be a nice change from the dump we'd slept in last night. When it came time to make plans for our trip to Oregon, I realized, much too late, that hotel rooms near Corvallis would be impossible to reserve on graduation weekend.

We'd ended up rolling into a ratty place in Salem late in the evening and falling into bed. The next morning, I looked in the hotel closet. *Where is it?* "Doug, this place doesn't even have an ironing board."

"Is your robe that wrinkly?"

I'd hung my gown in the bathroom, hoping the shower steam would take out some of the wrinkles, but no luck. I held up one of the sleeves. "Yes, it's pretty bad."

How can I be graduating from college and still not be prepared for one of the biggest celebrations of my life? I thought earning a degree would at least help me with the most basic life skills.

We had to leave for campus in forty-five minutes. There was a meet and greet for distance students before we all lined up. "Walmart has irons. Can you please run over and get one?"

Doug reluctantly agreed, but as he finished getting ready, I had another idea.

I dialed the front desk and someone with a heavy Indian accent answered.

"Can you please tell me if there's an iron and ironing board available?"

"Yes, there is. We keep them at the front desk for you." It took him a long time—too long—to explain about a rash of thefts. I thanked him and tried to extract myself as politely as I could.

"Who would want to steal an iron and ironing board from a hotel?" I asked Doug. Nevertheless, I left that morning in my Sunday best under a wrinkle-free graduation gown.

In the afternoon sun, while the lines slowly made their way

to the front, I wished I had opted for shorts and cute tennis shoes like the girl next to me. I adjusted my pantyhose again. They were chafing already. I'd already walked a marathon.

After the E-campus graduate reception early that morning, I had spotted a Mom-type African American lady behind an information table.

"Can you tell me where we're supposed to line up?"

The lady gave me a confused look. "You didn't read the email instructions?"

This was the second time I'd heard about this email, but I hadn't seen it. "I traveled from Tennessee earlier this week. I don't have access to my school email."

"Which school are you graduating from?"

"College of liberal arts."

She pointed behind me. "Okay, just outside this door, there's a map of all the colleges where they're lining up."

"So, not at Reser's Stadium?" My never-been-to-an-OSU graduation ignorance was getting on her nerves, I could tell.

"No, you're going to have to go find your college and the dean will tell you what to do." She looked down at my shoes—cute beige open-toed pumps I'd worn in my sister's wedding—but didn't say anything more.

"Thank you." I took a deep breath and stepped outside, my husband right behind me. College-age kids were whooping it up, laughing and talking. Overhead, the grey dawn had turned to a baby blue sky. *I'm definitely the oldest one here. I should be the cranky Mom-type behind the information table instead of asking for directions like a freshman who didn't pay attention at orientation.*

I crossed my arms and stared at the big map pasted on a wooden board. All the buildings were numbered, but as a distance education student, I wasn't familiar with campus.

I headed toward where I thought the college of liberal arts would line up. I saw sign after sign, several colleges, but I not liberal arts.

Where on earth was I supposed to go? Without my phone on me, I had no way to tell what time it was, but I was sure I was already late. I picked up the pace and headed back the way I came to see if I'd missed a block.

I caught up with another couple of girls who were studying a big paper map. "What college are you looking for?"

"Liberal Arts," one of them said.

"Me too!" I didn't recognize them from the breakfast reception, but figured they must be E-campus students as well.

"Here's Memorial Union. It's supposed to be up this way." One of them pointed up a street. When we arrived, several signs announced colleges, but liberal arts was nowhere to be seen.

"Hey, I see it, way down there!" One of them pointed to a group of people a few blocks down a road lined with tall, old trees.

"Good!" We took off, practically trotting to the sign. I arrived out of breath and waited behind the other two as they spoke to the dean.

When it was my turn, she said, "Name?" After I told her, she flipped through a stack of 4X5" pages and said, "Do I have you here? Are you sure it's college of liberal arts?"

What? Did I somehow screw up the graduation paperwork? What would I do if my name weren't on the list today? How could I break it to my husband that we'd brought the whole family to Oregon for nothing? I couldn't leave without that diploma.

"Ah, here it is." She licked her finger and pulled up one corner of the page to grasp it, then handed it to me. "Your number is 121. Find whoever's 120 and stand behind them."

Number 120 wasn't there yet, but I found the numbers

closest to mine. We stood for what seemed like hours in the hot sun. I took deep breaths to stave off dizziness. Eventually, number 120 (my blonde colleague) and 122 (whiskey breath) joined the crowd.

That was only the beginning of our long march across campus to the stadium. We walked for blocks, then stood still again for the parade of Ph.D. and Masters graduates. The final leg involved a steep downhill slope and a lecture by a man at least ten years my junior to watch my step. I was never so glad to get to my seat.

After two years of exhausting work, I didn't feel any smarter than when I began. I was as ill-prepared as when my mom dropped me off at the babysitter to fend for myself, or navigating a new step-parent relationship, unconsidered and unprotected.

Two rows ahead, a faculty member in a master's cape and funky hat motioned the students to stand. As they filed into the grassy aisle, each one briefly spoke with him, and then proceeded up the left side to the photographer. On the right side of the football field, a stream of people mirrored the ones on the left. A third stream of graduates filed up the center aisle. Up front, deans dressed in graduation regalia handed out black folders.

I crossed and uncrossed my legs again. After sweating for over two hours, the chafing had inflamed my inner thighs. As much as I wanted to walk up front to get my diploma, I also dreaded walking on the new blisters bubbling up on both feet.

When our row finally rose and filed left, the marshal checked each piece of paper we'd carried from the upper quad. "Are you Lyneta Smith?" He eyed me skeptically as if I'd errantly swapped papers with some other student, like identical twins swap classes with each other in junior high school.

Last time I checked. "Yes." I smiled, ignoring stinging blisters.

"Okay, head up there and get your picture taken." He pointed to the photographer, like I couldn't figure out how to follow the row of students who walked up the aisle, a single file line of ants.

This was it! I was finally going to get to hold that gold-embossed, black diploma cover in my hand.

Smoothing out my graduation gown, I stood on the photographer's tape "X" and smiled over my shoulder—not a "for the camera" smile, but a real-life, *this is the moment* grin. I was two steps away from the man handing out diplomas.

"Wait a minute." The photographer, a mid-30s man, came over to adjust my tassel. "Can we flip this back out of the way?"

"Sure." But can we get on with it? The diploma is right there in that man's hand. A dean dressed in full graduation regalia stood next to the box of diplomas, waiting for me to approach. *I'm next, so that must be mine!*

After the flash, I skip-stepped to the dean and thrust out my hand. My blisters swelled with each step, but I was going to enjoy the thrill of this moment for as long as I lived.

The dean's hand was a limp fish in mine. His "congratulations" sounded more like a sigh than a celebration. He did not return my smile.

But that was okay. My smile was big enough for the both of us.

I gripped the cushioned diploma case, rubbing my thumb along the faux leather cover as I headed down the long center aisle to the emptying stands.

Was my diploma really in here? Only one way to find out. Opening up the cover, I saw my name. It was official!

Now, I only had to make it to Doug and the girls. My smile looked more like a grimace than a grin, because of the sharp pains underneath the balls of my feet and the sides of my big toes.

I gritted my teeth, determined to make it to the car. First, there was ceremonially bedecking Doug with my gratitude stole and grinning for another round of photos with my degree. Fighting the crowds all the way to the parking garage. Smiling the whole way because it's graduation and graduations are supposed to be celebrations.

As we headed for the coast, we settled into a comfortable silence and our own thoughts.

I'd done it. The first in my direct line of ancestors to earn a degree. Funny, I didn't feel any more significant. I wasn't sure if God had even started redeeming my story yet. Was He waiting for me to do something before He could get started?

I'd been so busy with the end-of-year schoolwork blitz that I hadn't had much time to think about what I'd do next, let alone what God had said to me in the garage.

It wasn't like the awful childhood memories would magically morph into happy ones. But maybe He was talking about making a wonderful future. I'd been half-expecting the next tragedy to strike for a long time, but things had been relatively stable since Doug and I moved to Tennessee.

As the car passed under canopies of tall Douglas firs, I thought, "This must be what coming home feels like." This place, and these people had been the like the Shire in Lord of the Rings. All things familiar. Comfort.

Mark and Patti's beach house warmed our chilled bones with bright flames in the gas fireplace and a steaming cup of tea. As the sun set, I sank into the luxurious mattress and fell asleep to the sound of ocean waves rolling. It was the deepest, most peaceful sleep I'd had in at least two years.

The next day, I burst into the foyer of our old church, greeting old friends like a Labrador retriever, and getting hearty welcomes in return. I soaked in the familiar sounds and smells of the crowd and joined our adult Sunday school class and the service like I'd never been gone.

Even though it was Father's day, one of my friends had planned a graduation party for me in the fireside room that afternoon.

As I thanked my guests for taking a few hours out of their father's day, I remembered that I hadn't called my own dad yet. It was getting late in the afternoon. If I didn't call now, I might not catch him before he'd had too much whisky. Sometimes it was hard to understand his slurred words over the phone if I waited too long. I stepped out into the hallway and dialed.

He answered with the usual "Olsons," even though he'd lived alone for almost a decade.

"Dad, happy father's day! How are you?"

"I'm okay."

Okay? That wasn't like him at all. I'd expected his usual cheery, "Oh, pretty good."

"You sound a little tired."

"Yeah, I'm not doing so well."

Uh oh. "I'm sorry, Dad. What's going on?"

"I've been feeling pretty bad lately."

He'd used oxygen for several years by then, but he'd never complained before. A few months previous, he'd called me to say that he was letting my mom move in with him, because he needed a little extra help. At the time, I'd thought it was more that she was the one who needed help, and he was being nice to offer her a place to stay. After her sixth (or seventh, I couldn't remember which) divorce, she couldn't afford to live by herself.

I was trying to get used to the idea, but mostly I'd hoped that she would be quick to change her mind, as she often did, and move out again.

He told me he needed a rest after his sisters visited from California and Utah. They had been at his house the last few days.

"I'll call you again soon, Dad. I'm thinking about a trip up there soon. Okay? Happy
Father's Day."

"Thank you. Here, your Mom wants to talk to you."

Mom's cheery mood belied anything seriously wrong. "Guess what! I met some cousins I didn't even know I had."

"That's great, Mom." Maybe Dad just needed a few days to get well and then he'd be back to his chipper self, I thought.

Mom went on to tell me more about her long lost relatives and I half-listened while wandering the church halls. They'd painted the walls and updated the foyer with new furniture. New couch and end tables, silk plants, and a big, round information table. It looked much more spacious without the tall, rounded counter that had greeted members and guests for decades.

"You know what's sad, honey?"

I tuned back into what Mom was saying.

"Your dad says he might not make it through the summer."

What? "Why, what's going on?"

"It's like his body is just shutting down." There was a tinge of sadness in her voice.

He must have told his sisters that he was on a downslide, and that's why they traveled from Utah and California to see him. No wonder they'd made the trip. It wasn't often my dad's siblings traveled from another state to see each other.

"Anyway, when this is all over, I'm going to go out and

visit your aunt Marylin in California. Won't that be fun?"

When this is all over?

Mom rambled on, but I was stuck. *Might not make it through the summer?*

And "when this is all over." How could she be so callous? It wasn't a cross-country move or another huge chore we all dread. This was my Dad's life she was talking about. I couldn't wait until she was done talking so I could get off the phone.

Dad did sound awfully tired. I thought about my friends in the fireside room, eating cake and chatting. I should get back to them, but I needed to call my dad again soon to find out what was going on. Right after we made it home from Oregon.

And why didn't I call my mom out on her comment? Was I so used to her blatant narcissism that I always let it slide?

No, I just wasn't ready to deal with the repercussions. It would have been a huge fight—likely ending up with her hanging up on me. Who knows what she would have told my dad if I'd made her mad.

Someone had placed red, white, and blue bunting in the back hallway. They'd be hanging it up to decorate for their big Fourth of July service this week. I headed toward the sanctuary and opened the big wooden door. It was dark and empty, save a few lights up front. I let my eyes drift over to stage right, where I'd stood for so many years in the alto section. A twinge of wistfulness at missing out on the next week's

Our patriotic service had packed the pews of Newport Church of the Nazarene every Fourth of July. Locals and tourists alike looked forward to a musical salute to the United States Armed Forces.

There was a particularly sunny day, which is rare for Newport, crowds filled every pew. From the choir loft, I held a confetti popper at the ready for the big climax of the medley of songs from the four branches. Up in the balcony, other choir members did the same, creating a live surround-sound effect.

A slideshow highlighted service pictures of members of the congregation who've served. Some dated back to WWII, black and white throwbacks to another lifetime for some of the men who built the church building with their own hands, and a few in color from the Viet Nam era sprinkled in with the majority of photos like mine from more current conflicts.

As the grand finale of the show and the most powerful song ended, we pulled the strings, sending streams of confetti over the congregation in tandem with the sound of fireworks recorded into the soundtrack.

People looked up, their eyes shining with delight and surprise. As the sanctuary doors opened and hundreds filed out, delicious smells wafted into the sanctuary. All morning, some of the men cooked on the industrial-sized grill for the annual barbecue. We lined up to fill our plates with hot dogs and hamburgers, then we came back to taste the women's handiwork—pistachio pudding and brownies.

Like every year, I inevitably got the same comment from someone who saw my military photo in the slide show. "Lyneta, I didn't know you were in the military."

Given the surprise in their voice, I imagined them thinking, "You'd never guess such a heavy person could ever pass the physical testing."

But the running and pushups weren't nearly as painful as staying home. 5:00 a.m. revelry and drill instructors yelling day and night seemed easy and comfortable, compared to living with my mom.

Twenty years later, and I still couldn't get away fast enough. What kind of daughter can't stand talking to her own mom on the phone? Guilt pangs hung over my urge to flee. Things hadn't changed much since I was eighteen.

Chapter Nine

I hadn't planned on going into the military until my senior year. By then, I was thirty pounds overweight, and when the recruiter said I needed to lose that much by the time I enlisted, I started a fruits and vegetables only diet. It took three months to starve off the extra pounds.

My hunger pangs were minor compared to the chaos in our house.

After Kenny and Mom divorced that Christmas, we'd lived on his property until the summer. During that time, our house had been a revolving door of dates she'd met at Parents Without Partners social events.

Like any typical Friday night, I headed for bed while Mom talked on the phone. She was calling people to make final arrangements for a Parents Without Partners picnic the next day.

The next morning, she woke me up early. "Get up and get dressed. We're going to Hulett."

I squinted in the sudden-bright light. "We're going to Grandma Lil's?" *Much better than that stupid Parents without Partners picnic.*

"No, not today. We're going to a friend of mine's family reunion."

"Whose?"

"He's in Parents Without Partners." *He? Another man? Oh, come on! Let's just go to the lame picnic.* "Can I stay home?"

"Nope. Come on. Get ready. He'll be here soon." She ended the conversation by closing my bedroom door.

I stared at the wood paneling in my bedroom for a minute. This whole dating scene was getting old, and I hadn't even been on *my* first date yet.

I let out a sigh and flung off the covers. It would be useless to argue.

The friend of hers turned out to be Curtis, someone she'd never laid eyes on. He was on her list of people to call for the picnic. Apparently, they'd decided to meet each other in person after a lengthy phone chat the night before.

As a special bonus, we'd get to meet his mother and eleven siblings, plus their spouses and children (no less than forty people) in a town three and a half hours away.

He showed up driving a cargo van. As a co-owner of the local TV/Entertainment store, it was his only vehicle. My brother and I rode the long, dusty drive on the floor in the back. As we wound around the dirt roads, dust filtered in until we coughed and our eyes watered.

When we arrived, the reunion was in full swing. Obviously, his family had questions.

"When did you meet?"

And follow-up questions, with raised eyebrows. "Today? You mean you've never seen each other before?"

I wanted to crawl into a corner and escape into a novel, but I hadn't brought one. And there were too many people—they filled every corner of the house and yard. The day seemed it'd never end, though I'm sure it only lasted about six hours or so.

After that, Curtis stopped by our house every night. Things moved as fast as they had with Kenny.

In August, Monte and I stood with them during their wedding ceremony, like we had before. All of Curtis's family attended, and most of Mom's. We moved out of the trailer as soon as they could buy a house.

I often got in trouble for being disrespectful to Curtis, but it wasn't all teenage rebellion. My deep-seated anger flared up anytime I caught him leering at my chest, which was often.

It was such a stark contrast to his pious behavior in the flamboyant services in the Pentecostal church I was forced to attend—where Curtis would speak in tongues and turn on a buffoon cheerfulness.

I wanted to please God, but Curtis's behavior pushed me into doing everything he and Mom and said was of the devil. I listened to all the forbidden songs as loud as possible every time there were no parents in the house.

To get a song approved, I had to copy down each lyric (or find the cassette case label, if they were printed in there) for Mom or Curtis to review.

More than once, one of them would come home unexpectedly and confront me, red-faced and shouting, telling me to turn off the stereo. Each time I'd turn it down and give the proper apology, but inside be jubilant that I'd caused such a stink. I knew just how far to push it before getting any real consequences, but getting a satisfactory rise out of them.

A year later, they declared bankruptcy and defaulted on the mortgage. We moved to Skykomish, WA first (where Curtis worked at a gas station) and then down to Silverton, OR six months later.

Though we didn't move again until I graduated from Silverton High School, my last couple years of school were even more unstable than the previous ones. From the outside, our home looked like the idyllic place—big front porch with columns and a wide swing. We filled it with our idyllic-looking family, where parents led the middle-school youth group at church and kids studied hard in school. But inside that old, squeaky house, the foundation was already shaking.

In their third year of marriage, I'd already climbed into bed in my attic bedroom and shut off the lamp when my mom called up the stairs. "Lyneta, are you awake?"

"Yeah." I sighed, and then clicked on my lamp.

The stairs creaked as she climbed up. Before she even got to the top, the acrid smell of cigarette smoke stung my nose and eyes.

"Mom, can you please not smoke in my room?" I pulled the sheet up over my nose.

"I'm sorry. I don't know what else to do." She sat on the chair by my bed and puffed. "Curtis and I are getting a divorce."

"What? Why?" I sat up in bed, now fully alert.

Mom explained the diagnosis from her doctor's exam—an STD. Curtis at first claimed the residual, recurring symptoms were from his ex-wife, but he soon confessed to multiple affairs.

I tried to grasp what she was saying about him not having sex with other women. It was men, usually random strangers he met at adult bookstores.

As a teenage girl, I didn't need to know that those sorts of places had booths where strangers had random sexual encounters. As her story unfolded, I learned more than I ever wanted to know about the dark sex industry.

Mom's warning not to tell anyone both laid a heavy burden of the scandal on my shoulders without counsel, and reaffirmed the now-firm practice of making sure things looked pristine on the outside, even if the inside was a rotten, stinking corpse.

She had known about the cheating for awhile, but held out hope for their marriage while Curtis was willing to go to counseling in Eugene. It wasn't until she realized he was still hitting the adult bookstores a few times per week—during his trips out of town for counseling—that she decided to divorce him.

His leaving wasn't sudden like with Kenny or my dad. He drew it out for weeks, sometimes calling my mom from a homeless shelter, threatening to kill himself.

Living with just Mom would have been hard enough, but soon after she started letting two new men hang around. They drank a lot and stayed up long past bedtime, making too much noise for any of the rest of us to sleep. Under the surface of "pretend everything's okay," bubbled resentment. *How could she demean my dad for his alcoholism for so many years and then let this go on?*

I finally snapped one night. Late in the evening, dressed in pajamas, I sprawled out on my bed, doing homework.

The door to my attic room at the bottom of the stairs creaked open. Someone with heavy work boots tromped up the stairs.

The man purported to be Mom's new boyfriend appeared at the top. "Hey, Lyneta. Whatcha doing?"

I glanced at him, and then focused on my textbook. "Math."

"Oh, yeah? Is it hard?" He stepped toward the bed.

"No, I just need to get it done."

"Maybe I can help you with it." He sat on the corner, and then stretched out across the foot of the bed, propping up his head with an elbow.

The smell of beer on his breath turned my stomach. "I don't need help. I want you to go out."

He continued to try to engage me in conversation. He seemed happy and relaxed; his eyes were glossy.

I went back to my math analysis problem, hoping that he'd

just go away.

His calloused hands touched my foot, then slid up my ankle. "Hey."

I tossed the pencil on the floor. It bounced across the carpet as I lurched out of the bed, causing a wave in the water-filled mattress.

"Whoa. Hey, where you going?" He clung to the wooden frame to keep from falling to the floor.

I stomped down the stairs and into the kitchen. "Mom! He is on my bed." My sharp tone emphasized every syllable.

"Well, what do you want me to do about it?" From the tone of her voice, she was gearing up for a fight.

So was I. "I *want* you to get him out of my room! And how about out of the house, while we're at it! Why do you let him hang around here, anyway?" I emphasized the last sentence by throwing my arms out and letting them drop against my thighs with a slap.

By then, I could hear him bumbling down the stairs.

"It's not your place to say who comes here and who—" Mom's retort was interrupted by his entry into the kitchen.

"Not in my room!" I buzzed past him and stomped my way up the stairs, slamming the attic door behind me. The air reeked of stale beer.

It was soon after I visited the Air Force recruiter's office. Even before I graduated high school, I enlisted in the delayed entry program.

On the Greyhound bus to Portland to MEPS (Military Entrance Processing Station), I wondered if I'd made a mistake. Was I jumping from the frying pan into the fire?

Chapter Ten

Basic training lasted six sweltering weeks at Lackland AFB, near San Antonio, TX. We slept little, ate even less, and learned to follow every order to the letter. The first night there, I learned the most important thing about military service by watching a fellow recruit.

Don't cry. *Ever.*

If the girl with long, blonde hair was any indication, I figured best not to show any emotion whatsoever. She stood behind me in formation, which consisted of four straight columns of "rainbows," the nickname for recruits still in civilian clothes.

Two TIs (training instructor—the title the Air Force uses instead of drill sergeant) hovered on my right side, yelling stuff like, "Are you crying? Do you need a tissue?" and "Aw, poor thing! Did you get your feelings hurt?" The brims of their black campaign hats almost touched the back of my neck.

They were so close. *Were they talking to me? Am I the one who's crying?* My heart pounded faster and I fought nausea from the unfamiliar smell of thick humidity. I would've felt my face to see if there were tears, but we weren't allowed to move.

I didn't think it was me. They had also instructed us to keep eyes front, so I couldn't look around. The TIs continued their tirade until finally I heard the girl behind me sobbing. *Ok, so it's her. Just keep it together.* I breathed an undetectable sigh of relief.

We stood in formation for what seemed like hours before they let us eat a late-night dinner and climb into our new beds, covered in only sheets and a green wool blanket.

I laid awake for hours, listening to the voices of TIs carry from outside as they yelled at wave after wave of new recruits arriving.

During the day, TIs and student leaders alike would respond to any display of negative emotion with "suck it up."

It's probably important for a flight of 100 young adult women to learn to obey orders and follow a disciplined regimen without a lot of drama. However, my eighteen-year-old heart soaked in the false belief that my feelings don't matter, or perhaps it was mere reinforcement to that long-held childhood belief.

No matter what, just be tough and put up with whatever comes at you. I didn't differentiate between learning how to function as a military member and taking care of my own personal need to process emotions.

I had jumped from dysfunctional and unhappy to highly functional and overly stressed. We went to a briefing where a woman asked us to raise our hands if we missed home. No one did. But then she said, "No, really. Who misses home? If you don't raise your hand, we know you're lying."

All the other women raised their hands, but I still kept mine down. I glared at the briefing speaker, silently daring her to call me a liar. I didn't miss home one bit. At least not Mom's house.

On the way out of the briefing, I heard someone behind me whisper, "She didn't raise her hand." Though we'd get yelled at if the TI caught us turning around or talking in line, I chanced a dagger her way.

As miserable as it was pulling guard duty in the middle of the night, running at five o'clock in the morning, and having my actions dictated every waking moment, I still preferred it to the mess I'd left behind. At least it was a stable, predictable misery.

After basic training, I arrived in Aurora, Colorado on a snowy October day to report to technical school. As the bus from the airport pulled up in front of the squadron I'd call home for nine months, my belly did a flip-flop. Little did I know what would soon upend my already chaotic world.

I'd just gotten settled into a routine of classes, studying, and physical training when we got a four-day break for Thanksgiving. I went to visit my great aunt Helen and her family for the day, but the rest of the weekend, I had no duties. I planned to go Christmas shopping at the mall with my roommate.

Friday morning, there was a loud rap on the thick wooden door.

I opened it slightly, wet hair still dripping down the back of my shirt.

A female student on duty peeked through. "Airman Olson?"

"Yes."

"The commander wants to see you right away."

My pulse skyrocketed. "Okay. What for?" *Why is the captain here on a holiday weekend?*

Captain Craven, a formidable woman who stood at least six feet tall, had the power to kick a student out of the Air Force, and, rumor had it, exercised that power often. With her reputation, no one wanted to be called to her office. Ever.

"You just need to come now."

"I'll just put on my uniform and be right down." I started to close the door.

"I don't think it matters."

I yanked the door open again and regarded her ashen face. Something was bad. Very bad.

What is going on? I grabbed my room key and followed her down the hall and into the commander's office. No one said a word about my civilian clothes or wet hair.

Instead of sitting at her desk, the captain met me at the door to her office. She'd dropped the brusque demeanor I'd seen in briefings, and she seemed to be at a loss for words. "Airman Olson...sit down."

I started to move to her couch, but she stopped me. "Wait. You need to call your mother."

Uh oh. Something had happened at home. But what could have my commander so shaken up?

By the time I'd gotten to the payphone, a hundred scenarios ran through my brain. I steadied my pointer finger to punch in the phone number and then my AT&T card number. I held my breath until I heard Mom's voice on the line.

"Mom? What's wrong?"

"Honey, Beckie and the three younger boys have been shot and killed."

"What? What are you talking about?" Someone nearby was yelling—just freaking out. "That kind of thing doesn't happen in Wyoming!" It took me a minute to realize the person yelling was me.

"Clear this hallway!" The same clerk who'd summoned me now stood in front of the phone cubicle with her back to me, blocking me from the view of curious onlookers. "You need to clear this area. Now!"

A psychedelic wave of rainbow colors came back into order and I returned to reality. As I gripped that phone with white knuckles, I focused in her neat bun and fastidious uniform, willing myself to stay calm and present.

All of the people watching my hysterical reaction filed past until the hallway was empty. I finished the conversation with Mom and hung up.

Dear Aunt Beckie, my fun-loving aunt who'd taken us shopping and bought us nice clothes and taken us to the movies. By then, she'd remarried and together she and her husband had four children.

Murdered? This could not be happening. No one went around shooting people in Thermopolis, WY.

Some of the girls from my dorm had been called up to the lobby to receive instructions from the commander. I heard her say, "Make sure she's not left alone."

In a blur, I made emergency leave preparations and bought an airline ticket home. I called my Grandma later that evening. "Did they find the killer?"

"Well, yeah." She sounded surprised that I didn't know. "It was that Jaime. The police got a confession from him in the hospital."

Jaime, the oldest boy. The stepson Aunt Beckie had tried to love, but had grown more and more rebellious over the years.

Details trickled in little by little over the next few days as I waited to fly home for the funeral. Jaime had come home after partying all night and using drugs with his friends and gotten into an argument with Aunt Beckie. At fifteen, he pulled a shotgun off the rack on the wall, then shot her and his younger brothers. Then he set their trailer house on fire.

As a show to act like he'd tried to save his family from a fire, Jaime stayed inside for too long. Doctors hospitalized him for smoke inhalation.

The next Monday, the commander called me into her office again. "It would be my honor to take you to the airport."

Overwhelmed, I'd kept trying to convince myself there must be some mistake, and something this bad couldn't have happened. But for a commander of hundreds of people to take a couple hours out of her day to drive me to the airport? It was starting to sink in.

We drove in her minivan, making small talk. The whole time I prayed I wouldn't say anything stupid. As I stepped onto the curb at the airport baggage check wearing my dress blues, she said, "You look good."

I didn't know if that was a compliment or a command, so I saluted her, thanked her, and headed inside to catch the short flight to Casper, WY.

When I landed at the airport, the first thing I saw was my dad, leaning up against the wall. Though he smiled at me, he didn't move. I ran up to hug him. It looked completely normal, just a dad picking up his daughter at the airport.

Years later, I learned that when he found out his former sister-in-law had been killed, he sobbed and sobbed, but that day he seemed like his normal self. We drove the icy roads from Casper to Buffalo with the heater blasting and cigarette smoke billowing from his ashtray, much like the bimonthly drives from Sheridan to Buffalo when Monte and I were kids.

The days before the funeral were a blur. So many people I hadn't seen in years to catch up with. It was weird being out in public without my uniform. Since I didn't own anything nicer, I wore it to the funeral.

At the front of the chapel, they'd crowded four silver caskets adorned with yellow flowers. I hadn't ever seen children's caskets before. So tiny. My cousins had lived such short lives. Such a senseless waste. It was the first time I allowed myself to cry.

"No, don't cry. We need to be strong," Lenora, my mom's

younger sister, said from the pew behind me over my shoulder. Immediately the dam holding in my emotions shored back up.

As I'd been taught in basic training, "suck it up." I inhaled, swallowed the lump in my throat and sat stoically through the rest of the service. Crying was a sign of weakness, or so I'd been conditioned all my life.

Military culture enforced that notion. After I arrived back on base, I assured myself and others that I was fine. The captain and my first sergeant asked after me several times, and I told them I was handling it well. My week of emergency leave would have to be adequate time to deal with the grief. I had no idea what to do with it all, anyway.

Aside from one captain-mandated visit to the chaplain, I didn't go to counseling. I returned to classes and long workdays alongside people who barely knew me. I had only begun training for my job, and it was time to hunker down so I could graduate.

With a ratio of 20 men to every woman, I had my pick of guys for the first time in my life. I didn't let anyone get too close, though. If things started to get serious, I just found another guy to pal around with. It was a year-long state of flux with people leaving for their duty stations and new ones arriving every week. Graduation day came about a year after my high school graduation, and I couldn't get out of there fast enough. But I couldn't leave the pain behind.

After reporting to my first duty station at Fairchild AFB in Washington State, I began dating Scott, who would become my first husband.

On one of our early dates, we went to see *My Girl*, a movie about a little girl named Vada, whose father owned a funeral home, and her best friend Thomas, who died from an attack of bees. During Thomas' funeral, Vada climbed up on his casket and tearfully demanded that he be allowed to wear his glasses.

"He can't see without his glasses!" she pleaded.

The images of four silver caskets lined up in a row flashed through my mind. Vada was right. Thomas wasn't Thomas without his glasses. It was not unlike the moment I read the ribbon on Aunt Beckie's casket, misspelled Becky. A careless mistake that shot another jolt of grief.

The little girl's unchecked emotion sparked the surge of anger and sorrow I'd dammed up on the day of the funeral, and for the first time I let a torrent of tears flow. I stayed in the movie theater sobbing, long after the credits finished rolling.

Scott took my arm and led me out of the theater. I was still crying too hard to walk on my own.

"What is wrong with you?" he hissed on the way to the car, giving my arm a jerk.

"I'm sorry. I was just thinking about Beckie and the boys."

After dealing with his gruff demeanor the rest of the night, I stuffed my grief even deeper, determined not to let it out. No one could understand this profound sadness I carried, so I locked it up tight. If my boyfriend was mad for crying about their loss, there must be something wrong with still feeling it.

But underneath my crusty layer, the killings crippled me in unpredictable ways.

After Scott and I married and had our first child, Mariah, I went to the shooting range to re-qualify on the M-16 rifle. As the day of training wore on, my heartbeat became erratic, and I couldn't control my breathing. I fought the urge to flee. I tried to dismiss all thoughts of Aunt Beckie and focus on the target, but I kept picturing that hellish day in the trailer, the last day they'd be alive.

"Airman, which target are you aiming at?" The trainer's booming voice drew the stares of every other trainee and trainer at the range. I sucked in a deep breath and tried again.

At the end, he approached me again. "You didn't get a high enough score to pass. You're going to get to repeat training. And guess what? You get me again as your trainer." He emphasized his last point with a scrunched up face.

No I won't. "Yes, sir." *Jerk.*

I slunk out, wondering how I'd failed and why I couldn't concentrate on the target. After doing well in basic training M-16 qualifications, it never occurred to me that I could do poorly during annual training.

The incident shook me up so much that I made an appointment with the base psychologist.

As part of the intake process, I filled out a questionnaire; one of the questions asked about prior sexual abuse. Since the list was extensive, I went through each question as quickly and honestly as I could. On the sexual abuse question, I checked yes, thinking only of Kenny. Continuing down the list, I answered dozens of background questions about my mental health history.

Finally, the psychologist called me into his office. After introductions, he asked what happened at the firing range and I explained it to him.

"I'm concerned this could be a gun phobia," he explained. "I would treat it by gradually desensitizing you to weapons with repeated and increasing exposure."

Next, it was time to see the psychiatrist. He sat across from me and scanned the list I'd filled out. "Did anyone ever touch your genitals?"

I thought back to Kenny. Technically, he hadn't. "No." The bully in the babysitter's basement or the babysitter's lap didn't surface at all.

"I'm not really concerned about the sexual abuse thing. But the gun phobia could mean you're not mission-ready. We need to deal with that."

Because I was there voluntarily, I could choose to continue treatment or not. After another visit with the psychologist, I decided that, since I was planning to separate from the Air Force in a few months, treatment wasn't worth it.

I understood the need for mission readiness; any military member needs proper firearms training and the mental stamina to use a weapon if necessary. But the lack of concern for why I suddenly couldn't cope with firearms training after I'd previously been fine reinforced the belief that I wasn't worth the time and energy to find a way to help me deal with my personal grief.

It also reinforced the idea that what happened with Kenny and Curtis's creepy stares weren't a big deal. It steeped deep into my soul that I was powerless over anyone doing what made me uncomfortable.

After I separated from the Air Force, Scott, who still served active duty, worked swing shift (afternoon to late evenings), and I ran a home daycare on base. We lived about four blocks from the hospital where Mariah was born, in a quiet neighborhood full of cookie-cutter duplexes and playgrounds.

The days all blurred together in a less stressful routine—diaper changes, snacks, and Barney.

Out of nowhere, my routine turned into pandemonium once again. The children were just waking up from a nap when I heard, "*pop, pop, pop.*"

"What is that?" I asked Scott. "It sounds like firecrackers." A bit early, but not unheard of for the third week of June.

Then I heard a distinct *bang*. Once, twice, three times. Then a fourth.

"That wasn't fireworks. That was definitely gunshots!"

Scott peeked through the shades in the bedroom. We'd closed them to keep out the heat of the day.

I stepped outside a few minutes later to see if I could find out what was going on. A man in a white hospital uniform walked down our street.

"Ma'am, back inside," he said. "Stay in your house!" I closed the door, heart racing. Was a gunman walking the streets and firing on people?

I turned on *The Flintstones* as a distraction for the kids. Thankfully they couldn't read yet—the ticker on the lower section of the screen started a play-by-play report of what we'd later learn was a mass shooting at Fairchild Air Force Base Hospital.

I looked at baby Cameron, still asleep in the playpen. His mother worked for the base nutritionist's office, located in the hospital.

As the afternoon passed, I absorbed the news that twenty people had been gunned down just four blocks from my house, some of them in foodservice. I still hadn't heard from Cameron's mom.

A former airman had shot and killed people simply because they'd been in the wrong place at the wrong time. When Cameron's mom and the other parents arrived, they hugged their kids a little longer than usual. I stayed glued to the television long into that night, reading the victim list and listening to the news anchors' commentary.

My hand reflexively covered my mouth when I recognized a couple of the dead. The same psychiatrist and psychologist I'd seen. They were his first targets. He'd been angry with them for recommending his medical discharge and declaring him mentally unfit for duty.

The *pop, pop, pop* I'd heard had been the automatic rifle. The later shots were the security police officer's handgun. He'd heard the initial shots, ridden his bike from the back gate to the hospital, and shot the perp from seventy yards away.

As the community mourned, thoughts of Aunt Beckie came up. What were her last minutes like? I couldn't believe I'd never see her or the boys again. Such a sad loss for a woman studying to be a nurse so she could help people. I wished she could see the beautiful baby girl who shared her middle name just once.

I had long nights after I put Mariah to bed while Scott was at work. Since everyone else was sad too, I allowed my feelings to come and let the tears roll. With the uninterrupted time came a fresh wave of grief, not just for the tragedies on base, but for my aunt and cousins too. Night after night, I wrestled with my anguish until I sobbed myself to sleep.

"Why Beckie? Such a waste!" I said aloud.

Bitterness and hatred welled up for her murderer—I wanted him dead, like the gunman at the hospital. That would've been real justice. Instead, he was serving four life sentences.

I tried to study the Bible, but I could barely concentrate on the passages I read. I prayed, "God, please help me not to hurt so much from this!"

As I closed my eyes in prayer, I pictured a vision of Christ hanging on the cross. He was still alive, blood dripping down, and in agony. I hadn't yet seen *Passion of the Christ*, but I could imagine the brutality from my readings of the New Testament.

"Forgive them," he said to me. Only, instead of the sinners in Jesus' day, or even the murders, my sins played through my mind. I was reminded of the times I'd failed to obey, the times I'd been so far out of God's will.

Right then, I knew God was saying that I needed to forgive, because I had been forgiven. Christ didn't deserve one bit of that. He took that on for me.

I wept as I grieved for my own sin. I wept again as I grieved for the loss of my aunt Beckie, and my cousins. They didn't deserve that either, but I couldn't bring them back by holding a grudge. But would letting the killer off the hook dishonor their memory?

I thought of Beckie's fun-loving nature, and her tendency to play practical jokes. Before my parents split up, she'd made me a birthday cake and brought it over to our house for a party. That night, as she placed the 8X10" pan on the table, decorated with "Happy birthday, Lyneta," she said, "There's one piece with a surprise." After the candles and singing, and eating big pieces of cake with ice cream, she sounded disappointed. "No one found my surprise."

We pressed her to tell us what it was, so she finally did. "I ate one of the pieces while it was still warm from the oven, and filled in that corner with frosting." We laughed so hard about it.

She was always laughing. That was the first happy memory I'd had of her since the murders, the way she'd throw her head back and toss her dark curls. I pictured her happy and laughing in heaven. She wasn't suffering, and she wouldn't feel betrayed if I let my suffering go too.

I made the decision to forgive their killer right then. "Okay, God. If Jesus can forgive those people mocking and killing him, and if You can forgive all the horrible things I've done, then I can forgive Jaime."

In my mind, shackles loosened and fell away. Holding onto that hate and anger, I'd let him repeat his horrific act again and again. I imagined Beckie at peace and my heart unclenched.

I didn't tell a soul what I'd been going through, or how I'd finally been freed from the hatred. I kept up my strong, religious façade, working in the church nursery and faithfully attending services on Sunday and small group meetings during the week.

That glimpse of allowing God in because the pain had grown bigger than I could bear didn't last. I made peace with the circumstances and turned right back into a "do it all myself" Christian.

I didn't even consider going back to a counselor. Kenny's molestation, the babysitter's violations, and the bully's rape in the basement could never affect my life in the present. If no one I'd told had believed it was so bad, including the base psychiatrist, why would I dig further?

And so the memories lay dormant and buried for almost two decades.

Chapter Eleven

After a quiet moment in the sanctuary, I ambled back to my graduation party in the fireside room. Our Newport Church of the Nazarene family couldn't have been more different than the family I grew up in. Most of them didn't know about the murders or how bizarre our family dynamics were. And up until a few months before, I didn't even realize what an unhealthy environment I'd grown up in.

I didn't mention the phone call to anyone, but the conversation with Mom had clinched it—I didn't have a Mom like everyone else, someone who would support and encourage me. She had no idea how her erratic decisions and blasé attitude about Dad's health stung me. If she couldn't even afford to live in her own place, how on Earth did she think she'd afford a trip to California? To see sisters of someone she'd berated for his alcoholism since the day she left him. It made no sense.

I shook off my confusion and irritation and chatted with all of my longtime friends. With smiles and hugs, I circled the fireside room, thanking those who'd come, even Patti from Oregon City.

There was much to catch up on in the two years we'd been gone. As the crowd munched cake, we took lots of silly selfies. Those weren't even a thing when I lived in Newport.

My conversation with my parents rolled around the back of my brain. Would I ever feel I belonged among my Christian friends? I'd known them for years, but I think they assumed I was mostly like them. Would they still like me if they knew the dark pit I'd come out of?

Most of them had grown up in this church or other Nazarene churches. Some of the older generation had built the building with their own hands.

Would they still like the new Lyneta I was becoming?

For that matter, what would my relationship with my parents and siblings look like? I needed to get up to Dad's and straighten things out. In the two years I'd been away, nose to the grindstone, his outlook on life had certainly dimmed. It was time to fix that mess. I was planning a family reunion even before our plane took off from Portland to take us home.

I arranged with my siblings and their families to meet there over Labor Day. We'd be converging from Idaho, Colorado, Wyoming, and Nashville.

Then I made the call I'd been dreading.

"Hey, Dad. We were thinking of having a little reunion over Labor Day in Buffalo. Will that work for you?"

"Yeah, sure. I'll be here." After a slight pause, he added, "Here or in the graveyard."

"Daaaad." I drew out his name like I had as a teenager. I flashed on the time he attached a musical gadget to my turn signal in the '78 Pinto I drove. It played "Love Me Tender" every time I turned it on.

It was a good thing I was going up there soon. He had to be exaggerating, but he wasn't one for complaining. Mostly when I had time to talk, we spoke about politics, school, and who was doing what in Buffalo. He hadn't mentioned his health until he told me mom was moving in.

I'd sent him every paper I wrote for political science, history, and my writing classes. He commented on them all with clear understanding of the concepts. I told him more than once he'd missed his calling as a teacher.

So why the talk about the graveyard when his biggest health complaint was "not feeling too good?" Seemed a far cry from impending death. At any rate, if he did need more care, we could figure it out and get all siblings on board while we were up there. He was only in his sixties. His dad, who'd been dependent on a cane from my first memories, had lived well into his eighties. A strong man like my dad just needed to get his mojo back.

In the meantime, I had manuscript submissions to prepare. I was headed to a writers conference in Portland, Oregon, and though I'd had a "meh" response at a previous one, I hoped I'd made progress and some different editors and agents might like it.

I was to be in a mentoring class with the author of the sexual abuse book that had helped me so much. Surely she'd help me see how God was going to redeem my story.

In August, I landed at the Portland airport on a sunny day, and after collecting my luggage, I headed out to the crowded pick-up area where throngs of people waited. Cars, busses, and limos contributed to the choking exhaust fumes and just as I looked up, I watched the taillights of my hotel shuttle pull away from the curb.

No matter. I wouldn't let it dampen my spirits. And neither would it matter that when I finally got there, I got the parking lot view from my room instead of the mighty Columbia River.

I didn't even let the tepid response to my garden devotional get me down. Most suggested self-publishing, which meant, "no one will buy this book."

I still looked forward to meeting someone who knew what I was going through. A writer who understood the pain.

But the kinship with her I expected never coalesced. I didn't expect fast friends or anything, but at least to share the camaraderie I felt reading her book. I started to wonder what I was doing, going to conferences across the country, trying to pitch a book that had no pizazz.

I entered the dining room that night defeated and ready to go home. I'd catch up with a few friends then head for bed. The time change had my eyes drooping as it was.

I'd never heard the speaker before, never even heard of him, but in the half hour following dinner, my idea of God was stretched far beyond the one I'd had even after the garage encounter. I scribbled notes as fast as I could, looking up verses on my Bible app.

He started with a commercial portraying "the perfect dad," then read Psalm 27:14: "Stay with God! Take heart. Don't quit. I'll say it again: Stay with God" (The Message). He talked about how his son was always eager to jump in his truck with him every chance he got, just to be with his dad.

My dad had bought a green 1967 Chevrolet brand new that he still owned. I'd wanted to sit next to him in the bench seat just like that. I loved to help cut firewood or put out flags with him on Main Street on patriotic holidays. When he took me to work with him to his job building mobile homes, I beamed. He'd taught me to drive in that truck and I stuck to him as close as possible. He'd worked hard, even on his days off from work. Whether it was painting the house or changing the oil, he did it himself and enlisted my siblings' and my help. We built at least three rabbit hutches and a well house together. When he took a computer correspondence course, I was constantly at his elbow, asking questions as he soldered components to circuit boards for a 286 computer.

It occurred to me while the speaker was talking that I'd

taken for granted all the countless cribbage games, Uno nights, and sharing from giant popcorn bowls on the couch.

By the end of the talk, I'd vowed to be more grateful to my earthly Dad and my heavenly one. I wanted to know God more like the perfect dad in the commercial, not like the police officer I'd always had in mind, waiting to club me for breaking the law. The message was so perfectly timed and laser-focused on my heart. I could barely catch my breath.

I didn't linger over dessert. I hustled back to my hotel room and read Psalm 27 from my phone. I had done the "Read-the-Bible-in-a-year" thing dutifully for almost a decade, but the words now came to me like a fresh cascade from the mountain of God, whose character I'd so wholly misunderstood.

David was writing his story, but it could have been mine. As the youngest in his family, close relatives had often overlooked and devalued him. And though he'd made himself into a valued soldier in the king's army and found a close friend in his son, the king of Israel turned on David. The shepherd boy was now hunted like an animal, banished from the kingdom he loved.

My struggles weren't on a battlefield, but the trauma was no less damaging. I, too, was a soldier returning from war. My marriage counselor had confirmed the PTSD diagnosis early on. I couldn't shake it off. If God was going to redeem my story as he promised, how could I not yet be free from the terror of those memories?

My eyes kept landing on verse thirteen: "I'm sure now I'll see God's goodness in the exuberant earth." The NASB read, "I would have despaired unless I had believed that I would see the goodness of the Lord in the land of the living."

I'd lived despair, from January until God met me that May day in the garage. During the onslaught of flashbacks, I'd forgotten God was good. Or had I ever truly believed it? It wasn't written as a specific promise, but I took it as one God gave me personally that night. If David could be so confident he would see the goodness of God while he was still alive, then so could I.

The writing of 3,000 years ago came as a key to me, to trust God with my story and open my eyes to the truth: God is good, even in the darkness. David was a man after God's own heart who eventually led Israel into her golden years. Though I didn't expect to reign over a small country, I could suddenly believe He would use me and my past to bring the same hope and healing to others.

I needed to get studying and learn more about this heavenly Daddy I'd missed behind the stuffy God I'd always prayed to. I now had a new view, a coveted front row seat after having always watched from the wings. I could see glimpses of the truth that my story was playing out as He'd intended.

The following afternoon, I couldn't concentrate on the workshops, so I gave in to the beckoning of the river behind the hotel and took a long walk. Unhidden by fog, Mount Hood loomed clear in the distance with her snow-topped crest. I breathed in the crisp air and allowed the tension to flow out.

Had I only been hoping to be published to prove my worth? I wasn't going to find my value in a book contract.

"I want you to write your story."

I heard the voice inside again, an urging in my mind. "You mean like, memoir?" I had long ago given up on fiction and had never considered personal narrative. Why? Who would care? I was sure my only choice was nonfiction; my project ideas were Bible studies and devotional books.

I got a few minutes the next day to speak privately with my mentor during class and shared how her book helped me come to terms with what happened during my childhood. I told her about the flashbacks. "Do you think it's too soon? I wonder if that's what God wants me to do."

She nodded as if she'd heard the same scenario many times. "You *need* to write your story," she said. Her tone was firm but kind.

Yes, it had been a harrowing year, but my memories were fresh now and enough time had passed. Wasn't I living a redemptive story?

It was the confirmation I needed. I had my mission.

Patti let me stay a few days with her in Oregon City, a beautiful place whose name belies the fact that it's largely out in the country. On the other side of Mount Hood, more fogless days allowed me to rest for hours enjoying the view.

She'd lent me a book, which I spent most of the day reading. It began with a flashback, not unlike my own, popping up out of the blue. Heart pounding, I could feel the author's terror. And I was no longer alone.

I wondered about the connection between girls who suffer sexual abuse and mothers neglecting or verbally abusing them. Every story I'd read so far had those same dynamics. Desperate for love and unprotected, girls become vulnerable.

How could some mothers be so reckless? I wondered.

I thought about my own girls at home. If anyone even thought about doing something like that to them…I couldn't believe the rage I felt at just the thought.

In a counseling session with Aaron earlier that spring, he'd told me, "You need to consider the possibility that your mom was doing the best she could."

"No," I'd said. "I think my dad did the best he could. Not Mom. Do you know what I'd do to someone who touched my girls?" I spat the words. *"They'd be in mortal danger!"*

Doug had tried to stop me from saying it, knowing counselors are bound by law to report threats to hurt oneself or others. But Aaron waved him off with a good-natured grin. "It's a hypothetical conversation."

Maybe Mom couldn't have stopped it. But being so apathetic about it? That was inexcusable.

The level of anger I was starting to feel towards my mother was scaring me. I was a Christian. Weren't Christians supposed to honor their parents? Would I ever be able to get past this, let alone have a normal relationship with her?

I hurt for the author of that book. Her mother never offered any sort of apology or even acknowledgement of her pain.

I was so angry, I didn't know how God would heal it. But I was also thankful for a safe place to work out such hard feelings.

That night, over grilled steaks on the patio, the conversation turned to me. Patti asked how I liked the book and I related the story, how she'd experienced panic attacks and recurring memories of childhood abuse after turning forty. "Some of the stuff her mother said to her I heard from my own mom."

Patti's face fell and I saw sorrow. "I knew you were going through something similar, but I didn't realize...how awful."

Tears sprang to my eyes. It was the first time anyone had expressed agreement with what I felt about this deep, long-held secret. It was also the first time I'd let anyone I knew from church see into my silent reality.

Years before, Patti had remarked that she wanted to meet the "wonderful woman" who'd raised me. A twinge of guilt pricked me then for not ever thinking of my mother as wonderful. Now that this woman who'd become my spiritual mentor finally knew the truth, I at least had one ally in the church.

I arrived home resurrected. I had a new purpose, a new life

mission, to help people understand the incredibly powerful love Christ has for us. How differently would we live if we knew deep in our souls that we're His priceless treasures? As I began to make sense of all my pain, I knew redemption would come from helping others navigate the darkness as well.

But as I'd already learned from the other books, healing comes in layers. And I knew God still had a lot of restoring left to do.

Lyneta Smith

Chapter Twelve

As summer heat gave way to cooler September, Doug, Mariah, Katie, and I headed to Buffalo to meet my siblings and their families in Buffalo. We planned to stay in a hotel, but spend most of our time in the home Dad had lived in for over thirty years.

We'd flown to Denver, then rented a car for the six-hour drive to Buffalo. As Doug drove us through town, I marveled at how little it had changed since my youth. Main Street, with its old western false fronts and cowboy appeal, except for the brand-new Silverados and F-150s, made me think I'd stepped back into the eighties.

Dad's house sat on a hill overlooking Clear Creek a mile out of town. The giant living room window framed the Big Horn Mountains stretching over the golden-leaved cottonwoods below.

"I used to be so allergic to those trees," I told Mariah and Katie as we neared the house. "Sometimes I'd wake up with my eyes crusted shut." In the summertime, so much cottonseed blew in the air that it covered the ground like snow banks. Pulling into the driveway, the two years I'd been away seemed like a nanosecond.

With my brother, sisters, and their families there, the house felt cram-packed. We hadn't all been together for two years, the last time I'd visited Buffalo. We greeted one another and filled the living room, dining area, and back patio with chatter. It wasn't quite the same as other happy occasions when we'd gathered. Sadness hovered like a blanket.

For one thing, Mom was there. She was sleeping in Nicole's old bedroom, the one Monte and I had shared before the girls were born. No one else seemed to think it strange and I felt guilty for not wanting her there. But she was the intruder on our family gathering. I'd long ago accepted the divorce, but it was too bizarre to just act like her being a part of everything was normal. It wasn't. Not in that house.

But I also felt a twinge of anger every time I came across evidence that she wasn't truly taking care of Dad like she'd claimed.

Both of them were living in filth. A swarm of dead mosquitoes had immersed themselves on the stovetop in a half-inch of grease. The cream-colored tile in the kitchen was more of a brownish grey. Dust coated the living room furniture and carpet. Piles of newspapers and magazines threatened to topple from their stacks everywhere.

Dozens of garbage bags full of trash awaited transport to the dump in the garage, as did a gigantic pile of recycling in the back of Dad's pickup.

His old Chevy sat immobile in the backyard where he'd parked twenty years before when the water pump went out. The seat cover had rotten completely off, exposing all the springs. The avocado green color so popular in the early 70s had faded to almost grey.

Various relics from our childhood dotted the huge backyard, including two rotting rabbit hutches we'd built, still sitting up against the hillside.

Trees had long ago taken over the hill. It was now impossible to see the fence marking the end of the yard. Though beautiful, I was a little sad to think that no one could sled down in the winter, like we used to do on red saucer racers, or ride down in that rusty Radio Flyer.

Dad was worse than I thought. He couldn't even walk through the house without getting short of breath. Though he was happy to see everyone, I could tell he was worn out. He still mustered enough energy to protest when my siblings and I stripped beds and washed sheets, scrubbed floors, vacuumed, and dusted.

Mom commented that he wouldn't allow her to change his sheets and he replied that he wouldn't have minded.

She yelled at him that he was "making her look bad."

I had to bite my tongue and dig my fingernails into my palms to keep from telling her off.

Given his angry reaction to our pitching in to help, I didn't know which of them to believe. Either way, there was plenty of work to be done.

As with any family gathering, we pulled out cribbage boards for several rounds of games. That's when I discovered Dad couldn't see well enough to play anymore.

"It's like a big black spot in the center of my vision," he explained.

"Did you go to the eye doctor?" I peered at his face, trying to see where I'd missed a sign of eyesight failure.

"Yeah. There isn't anything they can do."

"Did you ask another eye doctor besides the VA?"

He shrugged and let out a big sigh. *End of discussion.*

Clearly, we needed to intervene. Mom couldn't, or wouldn't, even clean the house, and Dad needed more care than he was getting.

I called a meeting of siblings and spouses late in the evening and we crammed into one hotel room while Mariah and Katie cared for their younger cousins next door. More than a few tears were shed as we discussed our options.

My sister-in-law suggested a handrail for the bathtub. "I don't know how long it's been since he's had a shower. I feel so bad for him."

My brother suggested a shopping trip the next morning for a handrail, a magnifying glass on a stand for reading, and sweatpants. He had one pair. He'd never worn anything but Levi's, but he'd swollen so much from edema that his jeans didn't fit anymore.

"Maybe another shower curtain too," I said. "I don't think he's replaced it since before June died." Dad's second wife, Missy's and Nicole's mom, had refinished the interior of the house with a fresh coat of paint, new carpets, and updated decorations shortly before she passed away. That had been twenty years ago.

Next morning, I slipped out of bed while it was still dark. Mariah, Katie, and Doug were sleeping. Monte, Missy, and Nicole and I planned to drive to Sheridan to buy some things Dad needed and then go talk to him about improving his care.

As I got ready, I wondered why things had slipped so far during the last two years. Didn't he care about his health, his house? He seemed to have given up.

Well, I wasn't giving up. I hurriedly flossed my teeth and heard something pop from my front tooth and hit the porcelain sink.

Oh no!

A gaping, square-shaped hole. *Not again!*

I searched the sink for the crown. *Great. No hiding that.* I sighed.

My siblings were waiting. I found my brother's car and slipped into the backseat next to Nicole.

"How are you?" she said.

I smiled showing off my new look.

Her eyes widened. "Oh my gosh! What happened to you?"

I sighed. "The crown popped off."

For years, from third to seventh grade, I endured the same reaction from everyone. As if switching schools three times wasn't hard enough. And I'd gotten them fixed right before Missy came along, so neither of my sisters would have remembered.

"Didn't you fall off the slide?" my brother asked into the rearview mirror.

"Yep." I explained how just before Mom had left, I'd gotten not one, but two broken teeth.

It was at the school playground with two neighborhood friends and Monte. I leaned over the side of the metal slide, laughing at the neighbor kids and my brother below. The next instant, I plunged headfirst onto the asphalt.

I sat up, too dazed to make a sound for a few seconds.

My neighbor friends surrounded me in a semi-circle, staring down at me stunned. "Are you okay?"

I started to wail.

"Let me see your head." Monte helped me stand.

"We'd better get you home," the oldest neighbor boy said.

Blood dripped down my face as I walked the five blocks. We passed the Dairy Barn and a waitress ran out to offer a fistful of paper napkins. I arrived home a mess of blood and tears.

Mom and Dad both ran into the front yard having heard my wailing down the block. It was too late in the evening to call the dentist, so my mom helped me wash and rinse my mouth in the bathroom sink.

"Put this on your cheek." She demanded, handing me a washcloth.

At the dentist the next day, my parents decided not to fix the tooth and didn't mention it again.

A short time later, I was getting out of the car and Mom didn't notice . She slammed the door, smashing me in the face. The impact broke my left tooth in a mirror image of the right.

More blood, tears, but this time no dentist. They already knew there was nothing to be done but an expensive procedure.

Shortly after, I navigated my new reality of a broken home with broken teeth. In middle school, while others were getting braces, I was getting crowns on my front teeth.

We began reminiscing about our childhoods. Missy and Nicole were especially curious about things that happened early on in Dad and June's marriage.

I clowned around with a piece of Chicklet gum, pressing it into the hole in my mouth and trying to take our minds off this task we never wanted. After shopping, we geared up for the conversation with Dad that probably should have happened long before. We joined him around the dining room table, pulling our purchases from the bags.

With little time to lose, I launched into our ideas we had to help. Dad tried to turn the conversation to other things, but we only had one more day in Buffalo.

"Dad, just hear us out, okay?" I hoped the playful tone in my voice would draw him in. But he wasn't having any of it. Not cleaning his house, not doing his laundry, and certainly not buying him stuff.

He didn't want the new coffee table, a cheap one that came unassembled in a box. We bought it to replace the one he'd had for as long as any of us could remember that was literally on its last leg—the slightest pressure would cause it to tip and spill anything set on it.

"Dad, I know you don't like change. Just try it for two weeks, and if you still hate it, we'll put the old one back in the house."

"You'll come up here personally in two weeks and switch it out?" He challenged me like a teenager about to renege on a promise to clean the bedroom.

I returned to my practiced teenage defiance. "Yes."

The talk wasn't going well, but none of us expected him to accept without balking.

Finally, he'd had enough. When we brought out the walker and a shower chair we'd borrowed from the VFW lending closet he'd helped establish, he exploded.

"Take that stuff back! Take it all back." He half-stood, one hand propping himself up on the table, the other clutching his chest.

I questioned the wisdom of upsetting him further, but I also couldn't back down. I wanted to yell back, but I kept my voice even and calm. "You need this."

He lowered himself back into the dining room chair, huffing from exertion. Physically, he was beat, but there was fire in his eyes.

Missy broke in like she was talking to one of her preschool kids. "Dad, what do you say when somebody gives you something?"

We all chuckled. Of all of Dad's kids, Missy was the one who favored him most. And the one who could get away with the most.

"Thank you." Dad's voice dripped with sarcasm, but the edges of his mouth curved in amusement.

"You always taught us to do what we know in our hearts to be right," Nicole said.

"And this is what we know to be right," Missy added.

"There are lots of agencies in Buffalo that can help with some care, Dad," I said. "The Senior Center even has volunteers who'll come out and clean and bring you meals."

He glowered. "Your mom takes care of things."

"Dad." I lowered my gaze. He looked at me for ten full seconds before I continued. "Mom isn't physically able to keep this place up. And I can't bear the thought of you living in filth. We have to do something different." I wouldn't budge. I may have even given him the old definition of insanity of doing the same thing over and over and expecting a different result.

He stared me down and turned over his last card. "Don't you realize I'm going to die soon? You have to know that."

We sat in stunned silence. *Did he truly believe that?*

Finally, I said, "Regardless, until then, you need better care."

At last, maybe just to placate me, he agreed to think about it.

The next morning, we all stopped by for the last time before heading back to our respective homes in other states. He greeted me with a hard poke in the ribs. I tried to poke him back, but as usual, he playfully grabbed my wrist and held my arm away. He was still stronger than me, despite having to be connected to an oxygen tank.

After hugging my mom, siblings, their spouses, and nieces and nephews, it was time to say goodbye to Dad. I reminded him I'd be coming back to see how his care was shaping up soon.

As I made my way to the dining room table where he sat, I put my arm around him, and squeezed. "Okay, Dad. We're heading out."

He squeezed me back but didn't say anything. He looked up at me with...was that guilt? Sorrow? Regret? I couldn't tell. Whatever it was, he'd never communicated it before. It was a rare show of emotion. Despite the wrinkles and grey hair, despite the oxygen tubes running into his nose and the blindness, his eyes were as clear blue as they'd always been.

As I closed the familiar screen door, I willed myself not to look back to the picture window where he sat at the table. Something told me that was the one last look, so I refused to do it. I got into the car telling myself I'd be back.

As we pulled onto the interstate to head back to Denver, I had to suck in a hard breath to keep from crying. *Turn around,* I thought. *I can't leave! Please, we have to go back.*

I stared out the window for a long time, pretending to be interested in the sagebrush-dotted hills and antelope's white tails as they bounded away.

Doug put his hand on my leg. "What are you thinking?"

I laced my fingers through his, but kept my eyes averted. I had to say something—anything but what I was really thinking about. "I told them why I want to change the spelling of my name."

"Oh yeah?" he leaned back, smiling. "What did they say?"

"They were fine with it. I think they got that it was hard for people to pronounce."

I'd made up my mind to change it from Lynetta, the way my mom had misspelled my great grandmother's middle name. Dad hadn't wanted to name us after anyone, so they kept the spelling.

It'd cost a couple hundred dollars and a trip to the courthouse, not to mention an appearance before the county judge. But I was tired of feeling like my name was a mistake.

Soon after we arrived home, I summoned my siblings and their spouses via video chat. "We have to talk Dad into moving in with one of us. He can't go on living by himself. He needs full time care."

My brother was doubtful. "Dad's never going to agree to

that." Of course, Monte was right.

"We have to try."

"If Dad goes to live with one of us, then the others won't get to see him as often."

My response was not my most gracious self. "He won't be seeing any of us if he's dead!"

Monte lived an hour and a half away from him. If they couldn't keep up with his care, there was no alternative but to move him in with one of us.

No one could deny Dad needed clean clothes, something besides cardboard pizza to eat, and a lot fewer cigarettes. The VA in Nashville was connected to Vanderbilt Hospital, one of the best in the nation. It would be a lot more convenient than his current VA hospital in Denver. I explained all of this and then made the final plea. "Dad isn't at the end of the road. He's just hit a bump. We have to help him over it."

We all agreed to meet in Buffalo in October to talk Dad into moving. Three of us had room to take him in. All he had to do was choose where to move.

I would have told you I believed God could redeem my story. But I didn't. I was working hard to make sure I was there to fix everything. In time, I knew God would bring that breakthrough with my Dad.

Chapter Thirteen

September eleventh loomed cloudy and muggy; the humidity hung thick as I pulled dried plants and weeds from my garden. It was time to clean away the dead and plant a new fall crop of lettuce. Fitting, I thought, for the new life God had promised.

I hadn't felt the sharp pangs of memories since I'd returned from Wyoming. They'd been less and less frequent since that May morning in the garage. *Maybe I'm getting stronger*, I thought.

The lettuce would be my first fall crop since moving to the South. I breathed in the pungent smell of rich soil I'd cultivated myself all last winter in the compost bin. It was God breathing life into the dead, a picture of the work He was doing in my life.

I tossed another handful of weeds into the almost-full wheelbarrow. I wiped perspiration off my forehead and wheeled it to the pile, thinking about what I'd say when I called my dad later.

He'd be thinking about the first responders and the fallen soldiers in the wake of 9/11. In better days, he'd be up at dawn to put out flags along Buffalo's Main Street, like on patriotic holidays.

I went inside and picked up my cell phone from the dining room table. With butterflies in my stomach, I thought about dialing his number. It was 10:00 am in Tennessee, so 9:00 in Wyoming. He'd probably been up for a couple hours, still sitting at the dining room table working the Thursday crossword and Sudoku puzzles from the *Billings Gazette*.

During our last call, he'd rebuffed my reminder to check into the Senior Citizen's Center services available. Just more proof why I needed to get back up there.

First, I had to get clean. As I stood under the blast of hot water, I mentally checked off my to-do list. Walked the dog, watered the plants, finished the outside chores.

Then, I remembered. Dentist appointment! The phone call with Dad would have to wait until later in the afternoon. I had barely enough time to dry my hair and get dressed. I couldn't miss my chance to fix my chipped tooth.

A knock on the door, I opened it to see the pink hoodie of my daughter disappear around the corner.

"Did you knock, Mariah?"

She skipped back down the hall. "Yes. Uncle Monte called. I told him you'd call him back."

Probably an update on Dad. My brother had been going by the house during his commute to Sheridan.

"Hey," I said, when he picked up.

"Hi."

"How you doing?"

"Fine." He sounded funny. I knew he wasn't.

"What's up?"

The pause was only a few seconds, but it seemed to stretch out longer. I heard him swallow and struggle to speak. "Dad passed away this morning about 9:00."

Still in my towel, I sank down to my bed. "No." He couldn't be gone! "No, no, no!"

The next few hours passed in a blur. I called Doug and he came home from work. I called to cancel my dental appointment. Somehow, Doug managed to buy airline tickets, reserve a car and hotel rooms, and get us to the airport in time for an evening flight. We weren't sure if we'd even be able to land at the closest airport in Denver; a snowstorm had hid the Rocky Mountains, leaving half the town of Buffalo without power.

But the plane took off and landed again, and we slept in Denver that night. Doug and the girls slept. I laid awake trying to understand the electric pulse vibrating through my body I couldn't get away from.

On the way up to Buffalo, I wrote a eulogy and made funeral plans with my siblings on the phone. That night, after a day of sorting through old photo albums and boxes of keepsakes, everyone was gathered in the hotel lobby playing cribbage and other games. We'd talked to the funeral director and collected photos from all phases of Dad's life to create a slideshow. At one point, my brother had even instigated a snowball fight with wet, melting snow.

My throat hurt and I was exhausted. "I've got to try to get some sleep," I told Doug. He said he'd be there as soon as our clothes were dry. Too restless to play games or go to bed, he had to do something to feel productive, so he opted to use the hotel's coin-op laundry room.

Still grimy from going through old boxes, I slipped between the crisp white sheets. They smelled so clean. The pillow and the comforter were so soft and perfect, but sleep wouldn't come. I'd close my eyes, and my heart would clench in grief. Wave after wave of gut-wrenching sobs wracked my body and I couldn't stop shaking.

The image of the letters kept floating into my mind.

While searching for photographs, we discovered Dad had kept every letter we'd ever written.

"These are from you." My sister Missy handed me a manila envelope.

On the front in my step-mom's neat cursive was written, "Letters from Lyneta." I opened it and read one. October 16, 1981, with a return address from the apartment in Sheridan, where Monte, my mom and I lived the first few months after moving away.

My shaky nine-year-old handwriting covered both sides of a small piece of notebook paper:

Dear Dad,

Thought I might write to you and get a letter to my poor old dad. Thanks for the envelope with a stamp. I don't know if Mom has a stamp that I could send to you. I miss you so much!

I have a lot of friends over here and one of them is a little girl named Amy. Her mom and dad are divorced too. She is at her dad's right now and when she comes back, her mom is going to have a welcome home party for her and I guess I might go. It's going to be an over-nite party.

I love you, Daddy and I miss you!

xxxxooooo

Love,

Lynetta

P.S. I never really could make hearts.

A faded, misshapen heart adorned the lower half of the yellowed paper.

I'd had no idea how to find the right words to convey the anguish in my scrawling cursive.

And now I'd lost him all over again and the same feelings were back, this time with reinforcements, crashing into me like a tsunami of grief that had built up for thirty years.

It swept me back to a memory of one of our weekend visits, when he'd come pick Monte and me up from Sheridan every other Friday night after work and take us back to our old house for the weekend.

Our bedtime routine had always been a game. He'd carry us piggyback and dump us into bed. Then he'd scrunch the covers around us, saying, "Snug as a bug in a rug."

This night I was in no mood for a game. Instead of jumping on his back, I wrapped my legs around his waist and clung to his neck. Deep sobs wracked my body. He carried me to the hallway to my room, stumbling a bit. The closer I got to my bed, the harder I cried.

He stopped outside my door. "I think you're a tired little girl."

I nodded and quieted down, clinging to his broad shoulders and resting in his strong arms. I lay my face against his shoulder, breathing in the smell of car grease on his green Sinclair uniform and beer on his breath.

He stood there for a moment, rocking me back and forth, then squeezed me tighter. "No, I think you're a sad little girl, aren't you?"

I buried my face in his neck and tried not to start crying again. He swayed back and forth as I sniffled. My eyes drifted shut and I stilled. He stepped into my bedroom.

As he slipped me between threadbare, faded sheets, a live ash fell from the cigarette hanging from his mouth and landed in my open palm.

I jolted awake. "Ow!"

"Oh! I'm so sorry." He quickly rubbed the ash out of my palm and finished tucking the covers around me.

The sorrow in his voice prompted more sobs after he'd kissed my forehead. He stayed with me and patted my shoulder as I fought sleep, struggling to lift heavy eyelids and using what little energy I had left to cry. With his presence, the sharp pangs of separation diminished.

Then it was pitch dark; the hallway light wasn't filtering in anymore. I lifted my head from the pillow. The hand on my shoulder vanished.

With a start, I jerked awake. I wasn't tucked into threadbare sheets—they were crisp and clean.

Had he been here to comfort me just now? But that was impossible. He was gone. And no matter how vivid the memory, I'd never know that presence again.

The sun rose radiant the morning of the funeral. With the childhood memory of Dad's compassion still warming my heart, I began to get ready for the day.

In the shower, I found myself humming "What a Mighty God We Serve." It was more of an upbeat song than I'd expected to have rolling through the brain on the morning of my daddy's funeral. But I took it as a sign. Many prayers were going up on my behalf.

The day before, a friend had texted that she was praying for me, and that she couldn't imagine what I was going through.

"Thank you! It's more than I can bear," I'd typed back.

Angels bow before Him,

Heaven and earth adore Him...

The song buoyed me for the day ahead. Having Doug, Mariah, and Katie, as well as my siblings all together, soothed the raw feelings that had hit the night before. After the memory faded, I finally fell into a fitful sleep, waking often. Every time I would wake up, I'd let out a few sobs, and Doug would put his hand on my back.

This morning's sense of calm came as surprising contrast, but I'd take it as a gift from God. Despite the loss, God was good. I'd need the extra strength to get through the chapel service, the graveside service, and the dinner at the VFW hall.

In keeping with Dad's preferences, the chapel service was short. Lots of people I knew and some I didn't recognize filled the pews. Near the front, Dad's VFW buddies sat in their funeral uniforms. I spotted my mom in the back row, but didn't see her after the chapel service was over or for the rest of the day.

The family section at the front of the chapel was off to the side, looking out over the rest of the pews. We were seated hip to hip. Unlike Aunt Beckie's funeral, we opted to keep the curtains open. I listened to the homily given by a local pastor I had only just met, nodding along with everything he said. My brother, who sat down the row from me, fidgeted in his seat. As we planned the viewing and service, each of us included elements that were important to us. Yet sitting there, I slowly realized the sermon and hymns—maybe even the whole chapel service—were actually for my benefit.

We watched everyone else file out first before leaving our seats. One of Dad's closest VFW buddies was the last to go. He gripped my Dad's hand with his white-gloved hand, sorrow etched on his face. His shoulders involuntarily jerked up, as he succumbed to tears.

Finally, it was time for us to file past one last time. He looked peaceful, asleep. A fly landed on his face and I shooed it away. His hands, folded over his belly, would never be able to do that again. As our last act of honoring him in person, we would take him to the graveyard for military honors, and then have him cremated like he'd requested.

Only a few clouds dotted the bright blue sky as we filtered out of the chapel for the short ride to the cemetery. Hard to believe all the snow was melted and it was warm enough to be outside without a jacket since we'd flown into a blizzard two days before.

My siblings and I, along with our spouses, spilled out of the limousine. Since we opted for the eight of us to act as pallbearers, we pulled the coffin from the hearse and placed it under the tent on a set of rollers. Other family and friends gathered behind the tent as we seated ourselves on white folding chairs underneath.

In a ceremony I'd observed my dad serve in many times, the pastor stood next to the flag-draped casket and read the twenty-third Psalm. We turned to watch the color guard present the colors. Men my dad's age, wearing VFW uniforms and white gloves, moved into place with the American and Wyoming flags.

Five riflemen lined up and pointed rifles into the air.

Boom! I jumped, even though I knew the shots were coming.

Boom!

Boom!

The trumpet player lifted his bugle and began to play "Taps." It sounded more mournful than usual. I strained my ears to hear the echo player sound from over the hill until the last note faded.

In the solemnity of the ceremony, I focused more on how his death would impact everyone else. Buffalo had lost a patriot and a community servant. He'd lived the VFW motto: "Honor the dead by serving the living." My siblings and I, perhaps unknowingly, had adopted the stoicism he always showed when he bore the colors for those who'd fallen before him.

We turned back toward the flag-draped casket. The flag bearers, two of Dad's VFW buddies who'd been at the chapel service, walked somberly over to fold the flag. Even from my seat, I could see their faces heavy with sorrow. Though they'd performed this task over and over, it was still an easy job to bungle.

One of them shook his head almost imperceptibly and they unrolled the uneven triangle and began again. As they handed me the flag, I swallowed the lump in my throat, sharing these men's grief over their fallen comrade. The corners still weren't lined up quite right.

My brother whispered, "We'll fix it later."

The pastor opened *The Book of Common Prayer* and filled the quiet hush that had fallen.

"Ashes to ashes, and dust to dust..."

I slow-stepped back toward the limousine. My flurry of planning and preparing done, it was time to say goodbyes to friends and family. Together, we'd braved the final goodbye. After all the planning and travel, I felt my energy slowly draining out.

And a sudden chill had settled into me.

Chapter Fourteen

When I arrived home from the funeral, I put clean flannel sheets on the bed, the grey snowman ones Dad had gotten me for my birthday.

The last birthday present he'd ever give me. The thought brought more tears.

With a blazing sore throat and non-stop cough, I had good reason to stay in bed. But even if I hadn't been sick, I'd likely have ducked under the covers with a stack of novels.

Days rolled on, dragged out, and ran into each other. My life became coughing, reading, and sleeping. Since my girls were older and I didn't have a job, I found no need to get out of bed.

Finally, by day five, Doug set a bottle of water on my nightstand. "Maybe you should go to the doctor."

I pulled the covers up tighter. "They'll just tell me they can't do anything for a virus."

"You've been in bed for five days." His voice was gentle, laced with concern.

"I don't care." It came out sharper, more adamant than I meant to say it, but I didn't apologize. I closed my eyes.

Doug hovered for a moment more, then quietly stepped out. The door shut behind him with a soft click.

I woke up in the late afternoon, still in a daze. I blinked until the room came into focus. My dresser held stacks of papers and books, cards, lotion, and other things I needed to put away.

My gold graduation cord shimmered in the waning sunlight where I'd draped it over the mirror. Above it, I'd hung my ornamental tassel, orange and black with a beaver charm.

I'd spent the last two years on that degree and little else. Fat lot of good it did me. Two years for what? So I could let my dad's health slide to the point of dying?

I hadn't even visited him the whole time I was back in school.

The degree was supposed to help me do something significant. Be someone significant. Now I couldn't do anything. Didn't want to.

I'd always done something. In fact, the more invaluable I was to other people, the better I felt about myself. Whatever it took, I would never let anyone down.

As I languished in bed, I let my mind slip back to happier times, when I believed I had achieved my childhood dream of the picture-perfect family. A mom who worked hard enough and could hold it all together to give her kids everything they needed.

When we lived in Newport, our family was involved in the community performance of *Sound of Music*. Doug played Captain von Trapp and Katie played Gretl, major parts that required daily rehearsal. Mariah was a postulate nun, and I worked backstage wrangling young von Trapp actors.

Kim, the director, billed me as "backstage governess" in the program, a role I relished. She depended on me to make sure all the von Trapp kids appeared onstage in the correct costume for every cue. With some of these roles being double-cast, I had ten kids to wrangle and dress, being sure to keep the dressing room clear, help with hair and makeup, and launder costumes.

When we auditioned, I knew it was the wrong time of year to take on a big production. Katie had her end-of-year ballet recital coming up, not to mention all the other usual spring activities. But I was a mom people could count on. The one they needed.

Sound of Music rehearsal began at the same time as Katie's ballet recital. My goal—do them both. Perfectly. If I could pull that off, I'd be indispensable. Neither director would ever want to do a show without me.

Every year, the dance director choreographed a full-length ballet from a major literary work. This year, she'd chosen *Don Quixote*. The only problem was that she scheduled a surprise pick-up rehearsal at the same time as a scheduled rehearsal for *Sound of Music*. Intimidated and not one to negotiate a reschedule, I reasoned that at least both rehearsals were in the same building.

Luckily, I was able to shuffle my Energizer-bunny daughter back and forth without irritating either director. By that time, Katie was no stranger to the Performing Arts Center and soaked up every minute of it. I was soaking up what I loved too—the gratitude and approval of everyone who depended on me. Apparently, I could even pull double duty and make it look easy.

But that was another time and another place. Lying in bed, I knew my biggest fear was letting people down. It equated, in my mind, with being "bad." I remembered all too well my mother's expectations and harsh denigrations if I didn't measure up.

I realized I'd come to the point where I couldn't do anything anymore, mentally or physically. My energy to perform perfectly was gone and I was stuck, powerless, like the time my mother stood over my bed, threatening to lock me in the basement with the devil.

I prayed silently. "I can't do it anymore by myself, God. Show me how to live in Your strength."

Words from John 15 came to mind. "Abide in Me, and I in you." I thought I knew what those words meant, but I now knew I had no idea how to abide in God. *What did that even mean? Pray more? Depend on Him more?*

I asked Him to teach me how to depend on Him instead of working myself into a tizzy just to feel worthy of people's love and acceptance. I'm not sure what I expected praying that little prayer. But I figured it couldn't hurt.

By the next week, I was only getting nominally better. I couldn't shake the cough, but I also didn't want to go to the doctor. I knew Doug would insist if he didn't at least see some progress. So I got out of bed and trudged on. The next weeks passed in a blur.

Since my siblings and I had already arranged to return to Buffalo in October, we decided to keep those travel arrangements and use the time to clean out Dad's house and get it ready to sell.

We had three days to clear out a mess of a house. Few things he brought in had ever come out again for thirty years. I flew up alone and rode with Nicole from Denver to Buffalo. Six adults, with five kids in tow, checked into the now-familiar hotel late that night. The next morning, we arrived at Dad's house bright and early.

Mom had moved to an apartment shortly after the funeral, so no one had been there. I opened the door and almost gagged at the smell. Even though it was cold enough to turn on the furnace, an aroma of dog urine permeated the place so we kept all the windows and doors open. Fortunately, we'd have plenty of work to keep us warm. But it wasn't merely the physical labor that had me hot under the collar.

Dishes in the drain rack had caked-on food, hadn't even been rinsed. I knew they were Mom's. Kitty litter coated one of the corners of my sister's bedroom where Mom stayed. Her picnic table and metal fountain still cluttered the yard. Rows of canned goods labeled with her name lined the pantry shelves.

I calmed myself down and called her to ask about getting the rest of her stuff.

"I don't need to get it this weekend, do I?" The edge in her voice hinted at a challenge.

The old me would have said, "Oh, of course not," and simply shouldered the burden of getting the house show-ready for the realtor myself. Not this time.

I looked around at the overwhelming pile to sort through in three short days. "Yes, Mom. The realtor is coming Sunday. It's got to be cleaned out by then." Though I tried to keep my voice even, the firm edge in it surprised me.

"Wow, you're really stressed. You need to take it easy, okay?"

Don't tell me to take it easy! I thought. *No. Must remain nice.* "I'm good, thanks. I just need you to get your stuff. I'm going to get back to cleaning now."

I hadn't even mentioned the disgusting mess she left behind. But now she had me questioning. *Was I being unreasonable?* No. She'd made this mess and she had a month to move her stuff. I shook it off. That woman could get to me like no one else.

We had three categories: throw away, give away, and keep (to divide among us four). Since the dumpster would be delivered in the afternoon, we piled trash out on the front lawn and began sorting room by room.

Mom arrived later that day from her apartment to pick up smaller items that could fit in the trunk. As expected, she had plenty of advice about how we should go about doing the work, but no apologies or regrets about leaving the place a stinking wreck.

I kept working. My brother loaded her car with her jars of canned food and other small items.

She noticed a huge bag of plastic grocery sacks out front in the trash pile. "Those can go to the animal shelter."

Because we need more work right now? "Put them in your car and take them, if you want."

She huffed. "Try not to stress, okay?"

"I'm not stressed. We're just not making a trip to the animal shelter this weekend."

How could she turn my response to her unreasonable demands into me "stressing out?" She was used to getting her way by incorrectly defining my feelings.

When someone made a sandwich run, I offered her half of mine as I sat down at the table next to her.

She started to get up. "No, thank you. I guess you're too busy to visit now."

"Mom, I'm sitting down to lunch. You're welcome to sit here with me while I eat." I was getting a little tired of her trying to make me feel guilty for working hard to get everything done. My siblings and I had all traveled from our homes to get this done and she wanted us to act as if there was ample time to get it all done and "visit" with her, which was simply code for listening to her gripe.

She shrugged and scooted her chair closer to the table. We were alone in the kitchen, since my siblings and all their spouses and kids conveniently opted to eat in the living room or outside.

"Sure you don't want some?" I held out the other half of my sandwich.

She shook her head. We chatted for a bit while I ate. She talked about the new prefabricated house she planned to buy.

She mentioned a couple times how stressed I was. I bit my tongue to keep from mentioning the disgusting mess she'd left of the house when she moved out. She really had some nerve.

As I wadded the sandwich wrapper into a ball, she rose from her chair. "Well, I'd better go honey." She hovered over me. "Don't stress, okay?"

I stayed seated but looked her in the eye. "The only thing that's stressing me out is you keep saying that to me." I'd had enough. My tone of voice dared her to say it again.

Her lips thinned and nostrils flared. If history held, I was in for a shout-down. My insides clenched, but I was ready to give back as good as I got.

She took a deep breath, but seemed to deflate. Instead, she frowned and gave me two thumbs down. "That's not going to work."

She turned on her heel and walked through the living room. "Goodbye, everyone!" Her cheery disposition magically returned. She waved to them as she passed to the front door.

Not going to work? What was she talking about? She agitates me for an hour and then turns it around like I'm the one provoking her?

Unbelievable. I was never so relieved to see someone leave.

I sat at the table for a few more minutes, feeling alone, despite a house full of siblings and nieces and nephews. She had singled me out. I was the only one culpable for not spending time with her, despite the fact that her son and granddaughters were also in town. It occurred to me that this was the way it always was. I was the scapegoat.

We sorted, packed, and loaded for three days until the house was empty. In the process, we filled a construction-grade dumpster three times. I arranged for a local charity to come and haul away anything useful.

Once in awhile, there were tears over something forgotten and found. Every night we went back to the hotel sore, dirty, and exhausted. After showers, we let the kids wear themselves out in the swimming pool while we watched from the hot tub.

Despite the whirlwind weekend, I marveled at my new ability to be okay with who I was—how I was wired and my own personality. Living so far apart, I hadn't spent so much time with my siblings since before I graduated high school. Though our emotions were raw, we still found ways to enjoy our time together.

They were seeing the real me. On one trip to the dumpster, I accidentally tipped one of the plastic bins too soon. Rat droppings rained down on my head.

I swore.

"Lyneta!" Monte's wife was dumping her own bin right next to me. Laughing, she went to tell everyone that perfect Lyneta wasn't so perfect after all.

"I didn't think you cursed," Monte said.

"I don't. But rat poop in my hair is a special occasion."

We laughed. The work was hard and the reason for it was even harder, but at least we were together.

Little by little, every shred of evidence that we four children once had grown up there, that anyone at all had lived there, disappeared. At last, the house was empty, but still filthy. We stood in the kitchen, waiting for the charity organization to come back for the stove and freezer. Everything was done but the cleaning.

"It's going to take another day to clean this," my sister said.

"I think we should sell it as is." I leaned against the counter. "They're probably going to remodel it anyway."

The others agreed. We were out of time. And energy.

146

When the realtor arrived, she was amazed. "Wow, I can't believe how much progress you made!" I was grateful that at least someone appreciated our efforts.

I thanked God for His mercy. Not only did we surmount a major time obstacle, but four very different siblings had settled their parent's estate with little discord. Though I wouldn't consider us all very close, we drew together to honor Dad's wishes and get some closure on the nightmare we'd been through.

So this was what abiding instead of pretending looked like. It was messy. It felt out of control. But God had answered my prayers to bless our weekend and have a meaningful time with my siblings.

We took one last photo in front of the fireplace. All of the others we'd taken over the years had framed photographs and other baubles lined up behind us across the mantle. This one was bare.

Gazing out the front picture window, we marveled at the gold leaves against the clear blue sky and the creek running over grey and black rocks. We grew up in a natural paradise; we'd just never realized it.

Back in Tennessee, I made another appointment with Aaron, my counselor. I told him all that happened between Mom and me. "It's the same crap, different decade. All she has for me is criticism. The only way to get back in her good graces is to give in to whatever she wants."

"So do you want help learning how to get along with your mom?" Aaron sat with one ankle on his knee, relaxed.

"That's what I mean. She'll never change. The only way to get along with her is to comply."

He sat back in his high-backed chair. "Can you do anything about that?"

"No. But I feel guilty not wanting to be close to her."

Aaron nodded. "Look, all you've got to do is remember that boundaries preserve relationships. Whatever boundary you set will help you keep whatever's left of it."

I liked that idea. I had finally begun to accept that I would never have a supportive, nurturing mother. And if I could let go of my guilt, I could let our relationship be whatever it was without seething in self-pity.

Maybe I had more good to look forward to than I'd realized. Not that grief of losing my Dad would go away any time soon, but I no longer wanted to cower in the dark place forever. Maybe it was time to turn up the house lights.

Chapter Fifteen

I was writing at my desk when my cell phone buzzed. *Mom.*

A wave of anxiety washed over me.

I picked it up and stared at the word on my screen. The phone continued to buzz. *What kind of daughter doesn't answer when her mother calls?*

A flash of anger from our last encounter. I put the phone down. All my life, whenever she was angry with me, I did whatever it took to appease her, and was always grateful when she was back to her happy self again. This last time I hadn't done either.

After she'd stormed out of Dad's house, she came back the next day with a friend to pick up her large items from outside. She acted friendly and happy, chatting with everyone, but I had been coldly polite.

It would have been a lot easier to make pretend everything was okay between us, but I couldn't find it in myself. My heart was too frazzled. I simply made sure we didn't end up alone together, and spoke to her only when she spoke to me.

I hadn't stopped by her house to say goodbye before heading back to the airport, nor had I messaged or called her. I honestly didn't know what to say. Then or now.

I knew she'd just talk and talk, pretending that everything was fine. It was a lifelong pattern.

Our happy encounters aren't real, I thought. *She only treats me well when others are around to witness it.* I hadn't realized that before, not even in the counselor's office.

Taking deep breaths, I tried to will away the queasy feeling. I'd have to call her back later. Right now, I'd say something I'd regret.

Too distracted to go back to my writing project, I clicked over to Facebook. An article caught my eye: "10 Signs You Are a Victim of Gaslighting." Gaslighting. I'd seen that term before, but I'd assumed it meant purposefully escalating an argument. I clicked on the article and started to read. I was in the ballpark, but the word had a much deeper meaning.

"Gaslighting is a form of emotional abuse where the abuser manipulates situations repeatedly to trick the victim into distrusting his or her own memory and perceptions."

I couldn't believe it. That was exactly what my mother had done to me so many times. I clenched my fists and kept reading.

The term originated with a 1938 play called *Gas Light*, a story of a man who tried to make his wife seem crazy in order to cover up his secretive exploits in the unoccupied apartment above theirs. He convinced her she was hearing things when she was alarmed by footsteps above. When the lights go on in the apartment upstairs, the gas lights in the rest of the building flicker, including their own. He tells her she's seeing things— the lights aren't dimming.

The learner in me took over. I clicked on article after article, learning all I could. Since the 1960s, gaslighting has meant manipulation by deflecting or flat out denying the truth, causing the victim to doubt her own perception of reality. And there were so many stories about it—I wasn't alone!

Is this why I feel so frustrated with my mother? Because she just wants me to pretend everything's good when it's not?

Yes. My knee-jerk response to any situation was to do whatever it took to keep her from getting mad. Even adopting a version of reality I knew was false.

That way, she didn't have to take the blame for being critical or insensitive. She could twist it around and make everything someone else's fault.

I closed my computer and moved to the rocking chair. A light was coming on.

Had it always been this way with her? I thought back to the year Mom and Dad split up, the night my brother and I jokingly refer to "our jailhouse Halloween." Monte and I spent most of it in the lobby of the Buffalo police station, waiting for someone to pick us up.

A long time ago, I had brought up the subject with Mom. She'd said, "Yeah, I couldn't get to you because the interstate between Buffalo and Sheridan was closed from the snow."

But I hadn't remembered snow that year. Unlike normal weather conditions in Wyoming at the end of October, there wasn't a flake in sight. In fact, it was unusually warm. We'd even gone trick or treating without coats. But she seemed so certain. I'd questioned whether I was remembering right.

It was the first real holiday after their divorce. A dark pall covered our traditions that year—pumpkin carving, costume shopping, and trick or treating had all felt sad, perfunctory.

Even while picking out our costumes I was gloomy.

I grabbed a Bugs Bunny mask and a plastic costume.

"You want that one?" Dad stood next to me in the IGA grocery store as we made our selection from the few available.

"Yeah, I guess."

He picked up another one. "Here's a witch mask. You could wear this with a hat and cape."

I sighed. "This one's good."

Dad looked at me like he was trying to figure out what was

wrong. I smiled at him. "I'll be Bugs Bunny."

It didn't matter what I was for Halloween. I just couldn't shake the sadness. I didn't want to tell him, though, because I already felt bad for him. He was in such a rough spot.

Something was very wrong with him lately. I knew he was sad about Mom leaving, but he'd been a little more out of control lately. Instead of his Pabst Blue Ribbon, he drank amber liquid out of a brown bottle. It made him slower and he talked funny.

For some reason, we skipped our traditional trick-or-treating with the neighbor kids and drove to a neighborhood on the hill. The houses were much bigger and nicer in that part of town.

Dad stopped along each street and we'd walk up and down the sidewalks, ringing doorbells. Unlike our own neighborhood, most of the lights were off and very few people answered.

With one street covered, we hopped back in the big brown car. My brother and I were small enough to stand on the backseat while we drove, holding our plastic orange jack-o-lanterns. I liked the feel of the top of my head pushing into the solid roof, while my feet sunk into the squishy seat.

It seemed like Dad couldn't decide which side of the road to drive on. First, he'd been on the right side, then he'd veered left. I thought maybe he wanted to see how many people were home on the left side.

"Dad, why are you driving on the wrong side of the road?" Monte asked.

"Oh, sh--." He steered back over to the right.

Just then, I noticed flashing lights in the rearview mirror. I turned to look out the back window. "Dad, what are those blue lights behind us?"

He looked into the rearview mirror and let out another cuss word. "It's the cops." He pulled over next to the curb and parked the car.

The police officer asked him a bunch of questions and then told my brother and me to go trick-or-treating while he talked to my dad for awhile. I looked over my shoulder as we headed to a house across the street with a bright porch light. Dad was getting into the back of the policeman's car.

The older lady who answered the door barely glanced at us.

I moved to the left slightly to try and block her view. "Trick or treat," we said in unison.

She dropped candy in our buckets and said a cheery hello, but she continued staring at the spectacle of our dad getting arrested across the road. The blue lights lit up the dark neighborhood.

My ears grew hot. I was suddenly thankful for the anonymity of the Bugs Bunny mask. I could barely breathe from the embarrassment, but at least she couldn't see my face. We said thank you and headed down the sidewalk.

I didn't feel like trick or treating anymore. I just wanted the night to be over, to be safe at home. If Daddy got too drunk, at least no one there would see him. Hopefully he'd be done talking to the police soon so we could go.

We went to a few more houses and when we got back to the car, the police officer told us we were going to the police station for a while. I'd been there once before, on a field trip. The police officers had been so nice to us, showing us around.

Another police officer, a younger lady with black hair, wanted us to ride in the back of her car. I wanted to ride with my dad.

He was in the other police car's back seat. "It's okay," he said. "Go get in the other car."

The lady officer was nice, but strict. She made us sit down

and put on seatbelts. Thankfully, it was a short drive to the station.

In the front lobby, we sat on orange plastic chairs. Fluorescent lights buzzed overhead and reflected off the shiny white tile floor. I'd taken off my mask and untied the costume. The lady officer brought us a Coke and offered us more candy. For a long time, we sat in the quiet lobby, waiting for Daddy to come out. But he didn't.

Eventually, the lady officer came back by to check on us. We didn't talk much, just slumped down into our chairs.

Surely it had to be almost time to go. "When is my dad going to come out here?"

She gave me a sad look and said she'd get the other officer to come talk to us.

When the man came out, he knelt down on one knee and spoke quietly to my brother and me. "Your dad is going to have to stay in jail tonight. I've called your mom to come pick you up."

We erupted with objections. "Oh, no!" "Where is he?" "Can't we see him?"

"Your dad's okay. He's just going to sleep in one of the cells. He can go home tomorrow."

Tears sprang to my eyes. "But can't we tell him goodbye?" I didn't want to leave if he couldn't come with us.

He swallowed hard. "I'm sorry, no. I'm sure you'll get to see him soon."

We waited and waited, watching the door for Mom. I had wanted to go back to Dad's house, but now we'd be going to Sheridan instead. It'd be better than staying there, though.

And what about my daddy? Was he okay? What was he doing?

The year before, our Brownie troop had taken a tour of the

jail. Each cell had a bed, a sink, and a little silver toilet. The beds were orange cushions on a big shelf connected to the wall. They let us into one of the cells to look around. Everything was shiny.

"Here's where we put the bad guys," the police officer had said.

I knew my dad was probably safe in the cell, even though I wouldn't have wanted to be locked in. But was he a bad guy?

After the tour, the police officer had closed the thick metal door, which was painted orange too. It only had a small window. I wondered if Dad was looking out the window to see if he could spot us, or maybe sitting on his bed, hoping to get out soon.

Finally, after a long time, Mom's friend Jan breezed through the front door. "Ready? Grab your stuff. Your mom called and asked me to keep you at my house tonight."

But where was she? Why didn't she come? I didn't want to ask, because it didn't matter. I just wanted to get out of there.

We trudged out of the station carrying our wrinkled costumes and our plastic jack-o-lanterns. Jan drove us to her trailer house, and we went right to bed.

While my brother slept, I lay awake in Jan's back bedroom for a long time, wondering why my mom didn't come pick us up.

My phone brought me back to the present with another text. Doug. "On my way home. Need anything?"

The sun had started to go down. It was past time to start dinner. I'd frittered away my writing afternoon doing research. But maybe the time wasn't all wasted.

Now I had a name to put with what I'd experienced, a psychology term for the confusing way my mom made up her own reality.

Gaslighting.

I'm not crazy!

I'm not alone.

Thinking of my own girls as I prepared dinner, I had no idea why my mother wouldn't have rushed from Sheridan to pick us up at the county jail that night. It was a twenty-minute drive. If it had been my daughters, I would have been there in fifteen.

And why would she make up a story about snow? There was no snow that night.

And I could prove it.

I picked up my phone and typed, "weather for Buffalo, WY, October 31, 1981."

The high, 60 degrees. Inches of precipitation, zero.

Vindication.

So was she lying or just mistaken? I knew it wasn't the only time she'd come up with an alternate reality. It had happened a lot, especially when a situation made her look bad. But if there had been enough snow to close the interstate, why would we be driving in it? Especially for trick or treating?

I'd been stupid for believing her in the first place.

Over the next few days, I thought about all the times I'd been so frustrated with her. Now that I had a name for it, I could remember plenty of incidents.

But there was one memory that had nothing to do with her.

Before my Grandpa Darwin died, and before my parents split, my brother and I used to spend weeks at a time at their retirement home near Devil's Tower, Wyoming, where they owned several acres.

After retiring from the Game and Fish Department, Grandpa took a job as the marshal of Hulett. He would walk out their front door when the sun went down, donning his cowboy hat. "I'll be back when the bars close," he'd tell my grandma. When we woke up in the morning, he'd be at the dining room table, watching the deer and turkeys out the big picture windows, sipping a cup of black coffee.

During the daytime, he was free to fish from their pond, chop firewood, and take long walks across their property. And sometimes Grandma and my brother and I would go with him.

I learned early on that discovering an arrowhead in the dirt was the ultimate way to get praise and adulation. So I always looked hard for anything that glinted in the sun—flint rocks that Native Americans (of course, "Indians" to my grandparents) had chipped and filed into sharp points.

There were a couple important rules to observe: be quiet or you'll scare the deer. And walk behind the adults because of rattlesnakes.

One afternoon, the sun beat down as the four of us took a long walk. Grandma Lil was a few steps ahead of Grandpa's long strides, and my brother and I trotted behind them, struggling to keep up.

I spotted something black and shiny up ahead on the right. "Hey! There's something!" I leaped toward a dirt embankment where two black points jutted out.

Grandpa caught me by the shoulder. "It's nothing. Just a piece of garbage bag."

"No, I think it's—"

He yanked me around by the sleeve. "Stick close. You know what we've said about snakes."

Grandma's back was to us. Grandpa met my puzzled look with his "do-*not*-argue" look, so I knew better than to fight. I shrugged it off.

On the way back to the house, Grandpa made sure Grandma was in the lead. "It's the perfect time of day for snakes. You kids stay behind us."

"What's this?" Grandma walked to the ravine where I'd

seen the points jutting out earlier. She pulled out two of the biggest arrowheads I'd ever seen.

Grandpa jogged over to her side, scuffing the cowboy boots he always wore clean and polished. "Oh, my gosh, Lil! Those are spearheads!"

In a flash, Monte and I circled around. *I knew it!* "Grandpa, that's what I was trying to show you. I saw it when—"

"Hush!" He flashed me the look again and immediately I went silent. *Why was Grandpa so mad at me?*

My astounded grandmother couldn't believe her good fortune. Later, when retelling the story, she'd say, "All those years they were just buried in the dirt. I wonder how come the Indians left two perfectly good spearheads?"

Grandpa bragged on the phone about the spearheads Grandma found. They displayed them in the China cabinet next to Grandma's mother's depression-era China and their other priceless collectibles.

Later that afternoon, I passed through the living room, where Grandpa was sitting in the recliner. "You won't tell Grandma you saw those spearheads earlier, will you." It wasn't a question. He was giving a command.

How come I couldn't tell people it was me who spotted them first? It wasn't fair. "But, Grandpa, I found them!"

"No, I found them. I wanted to surprise your grandma, so I left them there for her to find. Okay?" He watched me over his reading glasses.

I hesitated, but finally I nodded.

He dropped his eyes back to the magazine on his lap. And that was the end of it.

Agreeing was the only way to get back into his good graces.

I'd worshiped him as a girl. I forgave him easily, and not long after that visit, he passed away. I was a teenager when

Grandma sold the property to move to Buffalo. While cleaning out the woodshed, someone found a receipt for two black obsidian spearheads, apparently ordered from a magazine. Why he'd planted them there for Grandma to find was the only thing that remained a mystery. It wasn't a malignant lie, but a major deception nevertheless, and one that involved bullying a little girl into compliance.

Clearly, a pattern of generational deception had been established early on. But how many generations did it go back? I knew from Grandma that he was known for his "whoppers," as she called them. There were many times she'd privately warn me not to mention to the neighbors certain things he'd said, not wanting me to out him unknowingly.

She'd never argued with him. So I learned to keep quiet too.

This was my legacy, the complicated relationship with the truth. The reality of it came crashing down around me. I could no longer pretend things were okay when they weren't. No matter how ugly the truth was, I needed to see it and know how it had made me who I was.

I'd created a story I wanted others to see, performing my best for them to earn their approval. Doing that had felt like the most natural thing in the world. And I'd buried the horrible things that had happened to be a shining, perfect example of the happy wife and mom, like the people I saw at church. I'd shoved all my fears and insecurities into a closet backstage, hoping no one would discover them.

But the truth had finally broken into my stage-perfect life. Despite all I could do to defend my polished production, I was so overcome by my memories I had no choice but to begin facing them after the encounter with God in the garage that day many months ago. And now, thanks to God and Google, I finally had knowledge and language for what had happened to me.

None of that helped with the deep pain of being lied to and unloved simply for who I was. But despite it all, I knew I couldn't go back to performing. My meager light could never light up the stage like the truth.

Somehow I knew in my heart the only way to be free would be allowing God to heal me.

But how?

I didn't know. I'd have to wait on Him to show me.

Chapter Sixteen

I skated through the holiday season like a ghost, working hard to make all the traditions we'd established happen. But it wasn't without spurts of tears. Christmas day came and went without hearing my Dad's voice on the phone or opening my mailbox to find the summer sausage and cheese package he always sent.

On New Year's Eve, I skipped all our traditional festivities and fireworks and went to bed early, spending New Year's Day, Dad's birthday, immersed in two or three novels. I'd lived most of my adult years removed from the reality of his alcoholism, but his absence now compounded the pain of missing out on so many simple connections we should have had. Instead, he was lost in a drunken haze. Though he never abused us, he did abuse alcohol, which stole him from us. And now it had taken him away forever.

When people asked what happened, I'd bite my tongue to keep from saying he drank and smoked himself to death. "The coroner said COPD," I'd say. "Probably from the emphysema." Their expressions of comfort didn't help. Deep anger still roiled in my gut.

I'd missed out on so much while he was alive, but now it had to kill him so soon too? Mom had always blamed his drinking for their divorce. And he was often too drunk to converse if I called too late in the day. Instead of tamping down the anger, I decided to feel it as much as I could, knowing it wouldn't last forever. If I needed to forgive him, too, like I had with Mom, then I couldn't just push away my anger. I'd have to work through it.

Between waves of anger, I would think of him and a weight like a rock would press on my chest. Tears would spring up and Doug would ask what was wrong.

"I want my dad to come back," I'd say.

Would the pain never end? I had crying jags every day all through the holidays. I wasn't even trying to cover it up anymore. The loss gave me permission to grieve all the injustice of childhood. Everything was not fine. And there would be no more pretending about that.

The bright spot was our new church. The authenticity and grace coming from the stage were real, and the people we were getting to know were so warm and understanding. I no longer dreaded going every Sunday.

In the middle of January, Doug and I sat in the crowded row of blue-cushioned chairs. I pulled my sweater closed and scooted closer to him. He laced his warm fingers between my icy ones.

Rain poured on the tin roof, and the thunderous sound almost drowned out the drums and guitars. I hoped that it wouldn't turn into freezing rain, not uncommon for January in Tennessee.

The pastor took the stage as the worship team stopped playing. "I had planned a sermon from our current series, but I'm feeling led to have a prayer service for healing instead."

He invited those who were suffering from physical and emotional ailments to come forward and kneel at the altar during the next worship song. I thought of my mental state the last several weeks.

As dozens of others streamed up the aisle, I leaned in to

whisper to Doug. "Will you go up there with me?"

He nodded and gripped my hand tighter. We made our way up front and squeezed in at the crowded altar. On the beige carpet, I knelt behind some who'd arrived first, and my husband behind me. The student pastor made his way down the line of people kneeling and spoke to each one quietly. When he got to me, he asked my name and then, "You need healing?"

Though I'd been freezing all day, a surge of heat overcame me. "I'm having a hard time dealing with abuse in my past," I stammered. How could I explain the fear of being worthless, or the attempt to find value from performing? Dad was gone forever and my mother would never be the parent I needed.

He seemed to understand. I could see the empathy in his face as he pulled out a vial of oil. "Can I pray with you?"

I nodded and swallowed the lump in my throat.

He dabbed some oil on my forehead and prayed for God to heal me completely. I agreed in my spirit, knowing that nothing I could ever do would fix my shambled emotions except the God who'd designed every aspect of me. No amount of striving or performing could ever penetrate deep enough to heal all the hurts. It was time to give it all over to God. And I would depend on Him from here on out to do it.

When the pastor finished, he put his hand on my shoulder. "Let us know if you need to talk more, or if we can do anything else."

My smile was feeble, but I was truly grateful. "Thank you." I followed Doug back to our seats. A reverent hush had come over the sanctuary. Even the rain had stopped pounding.

Despite the crowd, it was easier to breathe. The heavy weight on my heart had lifted. I'd just confessed the secret I could never tell anyone in church, let alone a pastor. And instead of the judgment I'd expected, I'd sensed compassion.

Thank you, God, for hearing my prayer. And for answering.

Soon, I found the courage to open up to our new friends. As we got to know people in small group and adult Sunday school, I shared some of what I'd gone through and what God was doing in my life. The more I shared, the more I learned that many others struggled with the same shame and worthlessness I did.

I wasn't alone. Others were suffering too, and I no longer felt left out of whatever God was doing in the world. I could see the good He was doing in others, and I knew He was doing good things in my life too.

In my prayer time, I felt God leading me to reach out more through writing. A year prior, I would have never dreamed of telling anyone, let alone for the whole world to see. But now I wanted to trust God to use my story any way He saw fit.

People started thanking me for sharing what God had done in my life and how I was applying Biblical truths. It became easier to talk about with each passing day. Instead of judgment, I received understanding. Instead of shunning, I found others related to me so easily. The message was loud and clear: people did need to hear what I had to say.

It wasn't my own need driving me anymore. My need to be known and admired had already been filled by God and a burning message was welling up inside.

In May, the discipleship pastor asked if I would give my testimony at a ladies' brunch and I agreed, even though the idea scared me to death. I practiced and practiced, and when the morning came, I arrived in time to help set up tables.

I thought to myself how different this was than getting ready for a show. Most of the ladies who'd signed up to attend helped in some way, bringing food and helping to set up. In my earlier theatre days, the director had taught us to preserve "the magic." She never allowed us in the front of the house in costume before the show. "You can schmooze with your fans after the show," she'd say. The goal was to make others forget we were just actors on a stage.

But here, the goal was to gather with long-time friends who enjoyed each other's company and be *real* together (maybe also to have tea and sweet rolls, but still). The "stage" was minimal, just a backdrop of two big, wooden sanctuary doors and an old podium. There was no need to impress anyone with magic. It was casual, informal.

Unstaged.

It put me at ease. When it was my turn to get up to speak, I tried to look each woman in the eye as I shared what God had done for me in the last year. Whenever I stumbled over my words, I gripped the microphone a little tighter, took a deep breath, and plodded on. They weren't getting a world-class speaker, but that wouldn't matter. I just wanted to share my experience, to relate.

I talked about our tendency to think that if we're treated like garbage, we *are* garbage and I challenged them to reject that and remember the truth. "How many of us would live differently if we truly believed God loved us as much as His word says He does?" Many nodded in agreement and a couple of people wiped away tears.

I talked about the princess we all knew who'd been born in a castle, but an evil imposter had stolen her and dressed her in rags, telling her she was nothing but a worthless slave and making her work from dawn to dark every day. But no matter how badly she was treated, nothing could change the fact that she was born into royalty. She was, and would always be the daughter of the king.

I felt a connection between the words and the experience I'd only recently begun living. And from that, I felt a freedom and confidence I'd never truly known, let alone expected.

All eyes stared intently and their energy flowed into me. I was newly confident I didn't have to pretend or keep a stage face on. I could share my true self and *that fact alone* gave me what I needed to deliver the real message I'd come to share.

"Romans 8:16-17 says, 'The Spirit Himself testifies with our spirit that we are God's children,'" I read. "And if we are children, then we are heirs: heirs of God and co-heirs with Christ—if indeed we suffer with Him, so that we may also be glorified with Him.'"

I put the Bible down and tried to connect with their eyes. "Our suffering doesn't mean He loves us any less. In fact, it's one of the ways He makes us more like Him. Some of us go around dressed like paupers when we should be putting on our princess gowns."

It wasn't a perfect or polished speech, but as I put the microphone down, the applause was generous. Afterwards, several ladies came up to thank me. Some of them even shared how they'd experienced similar abuse and had been hiding in their own secret shame. One asked for the verses. I knew God had done an amazing work.

On my way home, I thought back to my statement that I'd never be able to get up onstage and simply be myself. And yet today I'd bared the truth about every ugly thing I'd been keeping in the dark—and to church people, no less! I had shared the real cry of my heart for everyone to know how much God loved them.

I'd been surprised to find that the ladies in the women's ministry didn't have it all together like I'd always imagined. Some of them were broken like me, and they were exhausted from keeping their secrets in the dark. None of that shame belonged to me, and it didn't belong to them, either. And shining the light of God's truth on who we truly are as His children could remove that huge burden for all of us.

As I pulled out onto the highway toward home, I realized how far I'd come in the year since I'd had my encounter with Jesus in the garage. Maybe if I'd known what I was in for, I wouldn't have said "yes" to trusting Him with my story so readily. The thought made me chuckle.

Moving from a stage-perfect Christian life to a true-life relationship with Jesus hurt almost as much as the abuse, especially reliving it through the flashbacks. But instead of a destructive hurt, it was healing, like a surgery to remove a cancerous tumor. And the risk of not undergoing the surgery was greater than any other risk. I had to let the Great Physician do his work on my toxic beliefs—my beliefs about myself and about Him. The façade had to either come down or swallow me up in spiritual death.

As I passed by the rolling green fields dotted with grazing sheep, I breathed deeply, taking in the beautiful scenery. I thought about how much God had done since the days I vowed I'd never take the stage as simply myself. Performance-based faith was exhausting, but I couldn't give it up until God intervened that day in the garage, and then again as I grieved my past after my dad's death. I couldn't imagine what would happen if I left the curtains open to show the real work God was doing backstage—if people decided I was too broken to be of any value to anyone.

I'd been addicted to being the hero and receiving acclaim and respect—the false drug I could use to make myself feel worthy of love. The thrill of pulling off a fantastic production, impressing people with my spirituality, and everything I was *doing* was nothing next to the dream of finally feeling loved and worthy of that love.

I realized what He had in mind for me that day in the

garage. I was here to reflect His light, shining the truth by writing and speaking. And I'd keep sharing the message so I wouldn't forget it.

I thought about meeting one of the ladies at the brunch who was involved in another local theatre. She'd invited me to come audition for their next show. Maybe someday I would get back into theatre, but for now I wanted to make sure that if people saw me, they wouldn't see carefully crafted sets and elaborate costumes but the light of God's truth and what He had done in me.

I pulled off onto the exit near my house, thinking about how my life would be if it were played out on stage. My intermission year—2014—was the year I could have spun uncontrollably down a dark hole. But a divine hand had reached down and swooped me out just in time.

Me. Out of all the billions of people on this earth, He had personally come into my proverbial little dressing room and rescued me from the life I'd scripted. I'd had no idea what He meant by trusting Him with my story, but now I knew I could count on Him to show me His goodness in the second act. Though undoubtedly not without difficulties, it would be far less exhausting than trying to hold everything together by myself.

And that was a story I wanted to know the ending of.

As I pulled into the garage, I realized I was actually *thankful* God had let me relive all those painful childhood memories. Though they'd debilitated me, they were also the catalyst to let go of my performing and see the person He created was worthy of love and acceptance. There was nothing I could do to make Him love me any more (or less) than He already did.

He taught me how to lean on Him during those dark months, because I didn't have even a smidgen of power left.

Though I struggled hard against it, what I needed most was for my faulty self-light to go out in order to crave His light.

It won't be the roaring applause of men in our ears at that final curtain call. It will be a smiling Savior waiting with arms wide open. We can't imagine what we'll say in that moment. Thankfully, we don't have to.

His "Well done," will fill every need our hearts have ever known.

Lyneta Smith

Epilogue

What happens on family night, stays with family night. That's our motto.

At least, that's what we said before I became a writer.

The last time we played *Cranium* around the dining room table, on the last play of the game I found myself pretending I was changing my nineteen-year-old daughter's diaper. I exaggerated the steps of the process, much to the delight of the family. Their laughter almost drowned out her screeching.

"Mom! What are you doing?"

If Doug guessed correctly, our team would win the game. I looked at the timer—only a little sand left. *Come on, Doug! Say it!*

Just in time, he shouted it. "Changing a diaper!"

"Yes!" I fist-pumped the air and helped Katie up from the floor, most of us now spent from laughing hysterically.

Afterwards, during our prayer time, Mariah said she needed guidance to find a new job.

Oh, no, I thought. *She can't keep bouncing from job to job.*

"I agree," her fiancé, Chris said. "It's not a good situation."

Receptionist and driver at an auto mechanic shop had seemed a strange fit for her. But the look on Chris's face said this was something more than the usual work drama.

"I don't know what to do," Mariah said. "I took a customer home and was late returning because of traffic. When I walked in, Joe made a joke that I was probably giving a lap dance."

"What?" we exclaimed in unison.

I clenched my dessert napkin. "He said it in front of everyone?" It took a second to register, but the somber look on Chris' face confirmed it.

"We'll pray about it, but you need to put a stop to that," I said. "It's illegal and you have a right to work there without being harassed." I got up to take the dessert bowls to the sink.

"How long has this been going on?" Doug asked.

"It's been escalating since I started," Mariah said. "I don't know what to say."

"Isn't Joe your immediate supervisor?" Part of me wanted to go right over there and choke him. The other part wanted her to quit and not even give two weeks' notice. Of course, she couldn't do that, even if she could afford it. But no daughter of mine was going to tolerate blatant harassment, either. Not after all I'd been learning about how important it was to speak up.

"You don't have to put up with that," I said. "You need to talk to him and let him know that's not okay."

We prayed, said our goodnights, and I worked to sort out my anger as Doug and I cleaned up. He remained silent mostly, listening and affirming my defensiveness and obvious triggering.

Then driving home Sunday after church, Doug asked, "What do you think of going to talk to Joe tomorrow?"

I shot him a surprised look. I'd been prepared to let Mariah handle it. "What would we say?"

We came up with a plan and agreed not to tell Mariah we were coming. She'd be just as surprised as Joe.

On Monday, we went to the office. Two men sat behind the counter, but no Mariah. I'd expected the familiar smell of grease and the sound of torque wrenches, but all I smelled was new carpet. Behind the men were large windows looking out over the auto bays and the guys working on cars, the sounds muffled.

"Can I help you?" the one at the computer asked.

I smiled. "We're Mariah's parents."

"Mariah's out running a customer home right now."

"Actually, we came to speak to Joe," Doug said. "Is he here?"

The man's eyebrows raised and he looked at the other guy who put down his paper. "I'm Joe," he said.

Doug held his gaze. "Can we have a word with you in private?"

"Sure." He sounded anything but sure. Slowly, he rose and followed us outside. We stood on the front walk under a perfect blue sky.

"What can we do for you folks?" His confident customer service voice almost covered the concerned look on his face.

Doug launched in. "Like we said, we're Mariah's parents. She tells me you've been saying sexually inappropriate things?"

Joe's face went immediately white. "Yeah, I mean maybe some of the guys get a little crude around here."

"No, this was specifically directed at her. She said something about a lap dance?" Doug kept his voice even and businesslike and I was amazed at his calmness. I couldn't have mustered any of that restraint at all.

Joe stuttered. "I don't think there's anything like that going on. But if we've gotten carried away recently, we can sure—"

Doug cut him off. "I don't have any reason to believe my daughter would lie to me. Is that what you're saying?"

Joe stopped talking and started fidgeting. I was tempted to feel sorry for him. I knew Doug wouldn't let him wiggle out of this.

"Mariah's feeling harassed." Doug said and Joe sucked in a breath. He had just rung a bell with that key legal word, and Joe knew it.

"We don't mean for her to feel harassed," Joe said, chastened now. "We can talk to the guys and make sure it stops."

Okay, that's enough blame shifting, I thought. "She said his name was Joe. Are you the only Joe who works here?" I crossed my arms.

Now he looked beaten. "Yes," he said.

Doug took a step closer. "I know Mariah seems like a beautiful young woman to you, but there's something you need to understand. She's my little girl. Just because she's twenty-two doesn't change that."

His expression shifted from nervous-defensive to pained. "I see what you mean. I have a little girl myself. She's three."

"So we have an understanding? Mariah needs to be treated with respect."

"Absolutely." His relief was palpable.

I smiled and shook his hand. "Okay, Joe. Thanks for listening."

Doug followed suit and offered his hand too. "Have a great day."

I was glad my back was to Joe as we walked to the parking lot, because I couldn't contain my grin. Was it bad that I'd so enjoyed seeing him squirm?

Doug opened the car door for me.

"I think he peed his pants a little," I said.

Doug laughed. "Yep, he probably did."

We decided to take a drive. Doug was quiet, and I knew he was probably processing. Finally, he said, "I hope he thinks about what I said."

"I think the idea that Mariah is your little girl hit home."

"He's not a bad guy. He's just learned that women are objects. He's probably never thought that every woman is someone's little girl."

I giggled. "Well, he's thinking about it today."

Doug smiled and took my hand. We drove the two-lane highway through the green rolling hills of Natchez Trace, and I settled down into the leather seat and pointed out the purple flowering trees. We talked about the future—our changing family with the upcoming addition of Chris as son-in-law that summer, our new ministry focus, and new life as empty-nesters. I took a deep breath and drank in the beauty of God's creation. *And if pin oaks and pine trees are this magnificent*, I thought, *how beautiful must God think we are, the first fruits of His creation.*

How many others like Joe needed to realize the inherent value of women, of people? It was likely he didn't even realize his own value—that he wasn't just an instinctual animal, doing and thinking whatever feels good, but designed with a free will and a unique purpose. I wondered if he knew the Inspirer calling it all to life within him.

Was all of that God's reason for pulling me off the stage for that intermission year, so I could understand my real purpose? My role for the second act could be just this, to ask, "How differently would we live if we truly believed how much God loves us? Who would we be if we really understood our inherent value? And how would we treat people if we really knew their inherent value?"

After so many years, of fearing the call for "Places!" I'm finally settling into the knowledge of what it means to stand up in the assurance of God's unwavering love. I thank God for Doug and my family, and even the intermission of my life—the semicolon year, and the following recovery year—though I'm so happy they came to a close. And I now have a distinct message to share with others as I live out the second act, basking in the true light.

I know He sees me.

He values *me* above all His marvelous creation. He didn't create us to suffer, but He'll use it all to prepare us for our purpose, if we'll stop performing and let Him do it.

It's never easy going back onstage after a disastrous first act. But He's got this story.

And it's His smile I see out there in the darkness.

Note from the Author

Did my story resonate with you or inspire you? Consider leaving a review on Amazon and Goodreads. Authors count on reviews to help other readers find great books. Much appreciated!

I love getting messages from people like you who've been blessed in some way by what I've written. If that's you, please reach out to me at Lyneta@LynetaSmith.com.

Acknowledgements

Even though writing is a solitary activity, it takes a whole lot of love and support to publish a book! I'm so grateful to you, my readers, for sharing in my story.

I'm also grateful to so many others, who sacrificially gave of their time and talents to make this book happen:

Mick Silva, for your hours and hours of coaching, for encouraging me to write bravely, and for believing I could do this, even when I wasn't so sure. Without you and Sheri, I doubt this book could have been created.

Sherri Wilson Johnson for all of your expertise and beautiful design work.

Ramona Richards for reading and generously sharing your insights. Every suggestion was gold.

Elaine Cooper, your encouragement, and the bravery you showed to write your own memoir fueled me through this project.

Maresa, Tammie, and Cindi (my Triple Gs), You kept me going through the hard parts and celebrated every win with me. Your insights made this a much better book.

Mary DeMuth, for being the first to assure me I wasn't alone and for encouraging me to start writing this book. Without you, I don't know how my healing journey could have even begun. Thanks, as always, for your beautiful words of hope and encouragement.

Tonya Kubo, for championing this project and bringing all the excitement to my publishing journey. You're a delight to work with!

Kathi Lipp, where would I be without your wisdom, inspiration, and passion for serving your readers? I'm so grateful for your mentorship. And even more grateful for your generous friendship. Everyone needs a champion like you on their side.

The rest of the team at Kathi Lipp, LLC, you've been most generous with your support and offers to help. I'm grateful to get to work with such an excellent team.

SHOTS Writers Collective (Melissa, Amy, Krista, Lydia, and Rachel), for all of your ideas and encouragement. Early morning write-ins are the best cure for looming deadlines.

Blue Ridge Mountains Christian Writers Conference faculty, especially Edie Melson, DiAnn Mills, and Eva Marie Everson. Your commitment to equipping writers has taught me so much about writing and the business of publishing.

Patti and Mark Foley, for sharing your home and hearts—a place where I can always run for comfort and healing. Patti, for being my biggest cheerleader!

Linda, Teri, Patti, Doris, and Sandy (aka The Koffee Klatch), your friendship and discipleship shaped me in ways that even I probably don't recognize. Much of what I understand about the Bible and following Jesus, I learned from you.

The wonderful staff at Grace Church of the Nazarene, especially Sue Purvis and Derek Whitten, for your compassionate service and care. You demonstrate what Jesus meant when He told Peter to feed His lambs.

My siblings, Monte, Missy, and Nicole, for all the ways you've overcome the hard stuff and how much you've invested in your beautiful families. It warms my heart to see you passing on a legacy of love and stability in your homes. Your support on this project has meant everything to me.

Stephanie, Tiffany, Mariah, and Katie for all the inspiring ways you take on life and for the light and beauty you add to this world.

Doug, you're the string to my kite. I wouldn't want to fly through life with anyone but you--best traveling buddy ever! It's hard enough to live with a writer, but you walked through the fire with me without even flinching.

Most of all, thanks to my loving Heavenly Father, who never gave up on me even when I lost my way. You showed me that the existence of evil doesn't eliminate Your goodness—it illuminates it when we trust You with our story.

About the Author

Lyneta Smith and her husband are happy empty nesters living in the Pacific Northwest. When she's not writing or editing, you can find her down at the local coffee shop gabbing with friends, teaching Bible study, or snuggled up with a good book.

She'd love to connect with you!

www.LynetaSmith.com

https://www.facebook.com/LynetaS

https://twitter.com/LynetaS

https://www.instagram.com/lyneta_smith/

Lyneta@LynetaSmith.com

Made in the USA
Monee, IL
21 April 2021